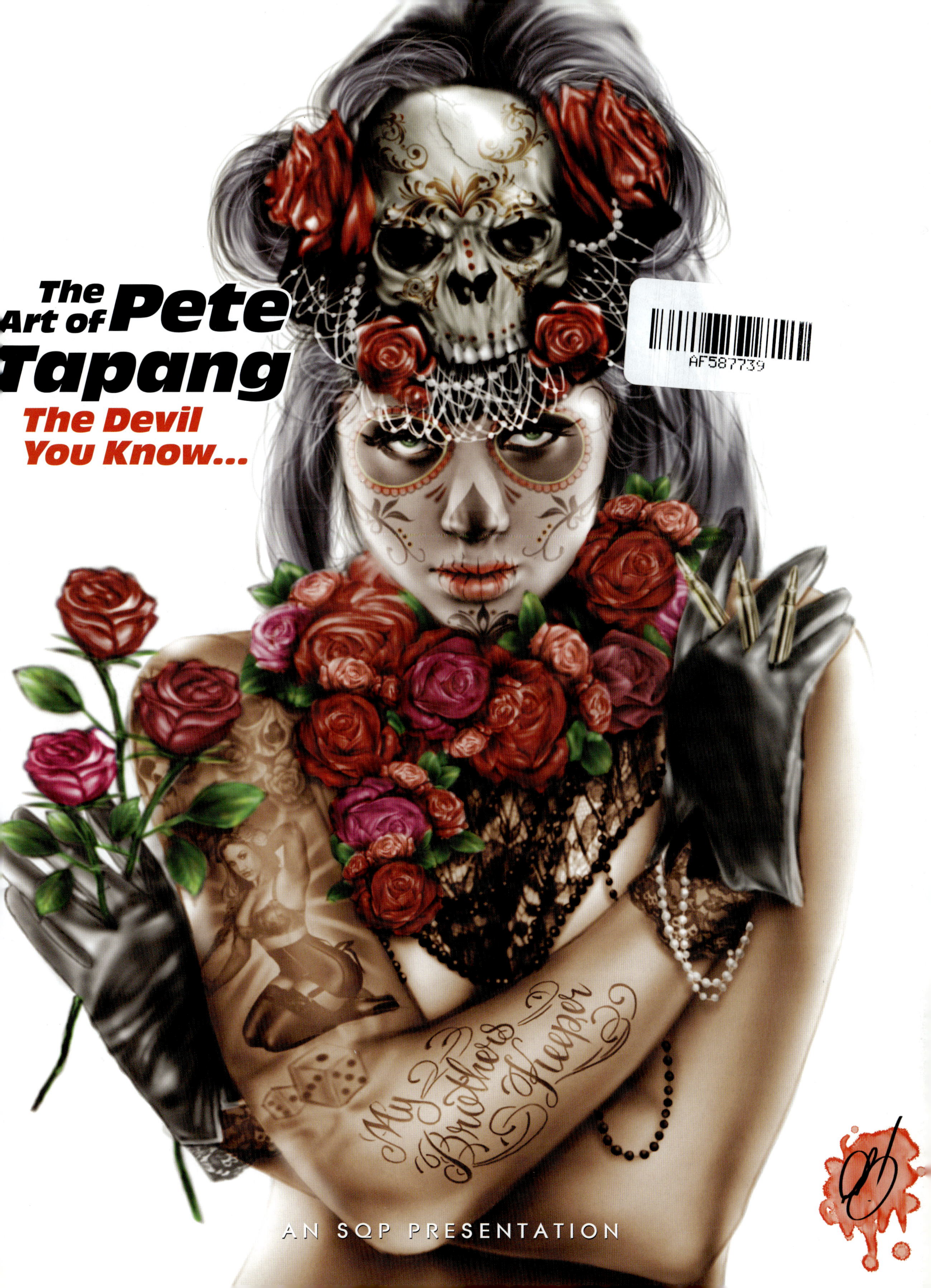
The Art of Pete Tapang
The Devil You Know...
My Brother's Keeper
AN SQP PRESENTATION

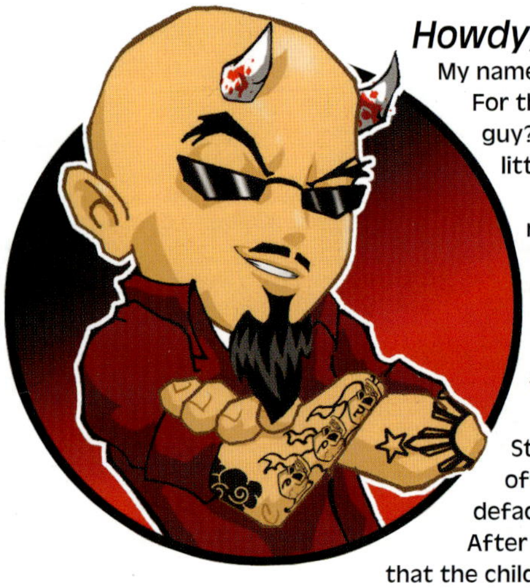

***Howdy,***

My name is Pete Tapang.

For those of you who are thinking to yourselves "Who the hell is this guy?" and "Oh dear god!!! Words in an art book??!?" I'm going to tell you a little story.

On the morning of June 23rd, 1980 as the moon sank and the sun rose in the city known as Frankfurt Germany, a small creature... or er... child was introduced to the world. This strange child, created from a school teacher and a soldier lifted his right eyebrow and grinned as he was born with a great power... a power only bestowed upon heroes, champions, and legends alike... a power, that would soon forever change the world.

As the boy grew older, he began to display his power in school. Still young and unable to control his magnificent gift, teachers often scolded him in dismay as he used his god like abilities to deface literature, desks, and people's reputations.

After months of recklessly displaying his gift, it was then thought that the child's abilities may be used for a purpose and he was later introduced to several teachers to help him learn to control and properly utilize his amazing power.

As many years passed the boy began to grow tired of instructors asking him to create simple circles and squares over and over again. The boy knew that his powers were growing stronger and if he did not use them to their full potential he would soon grow weak. "When?" He asked. "When would these teachers allow me to use this amazing gift?"

The child soon grew into a young man. Bored and angry, he felt that his powers were too strong and there was nothing else a teacher could offer him and began to rebel against his instructors. Circles, squares and flowers? Screw that, the boy created super heroes, aliens, robots with lasers attached to what now thinking about it looked like nipples.

They asked him to create a vase, he created a bong. They asked him to create two everyday objects together in harmony; he created a cow... not just an ordinary cow, but a cow being eaten alive by rabbits. Not only did he win the affections of his fellow school mates, he also won a permanent place in the principal's office with failing grades.

One day, the young man was introduced to a new instructor known as Mr. O'Connor. This instructor was different than the rest. He allowed the boy to use his power any way he wanted and didn't instruct him on what to create, but guided him on how to perfect his skill.

After finishing school, the young man decided to serve his country the same way his father did and joined the army.

After the young man served his time and a few years had passed, the young man realized he was a fool for thinking he was the best and there was nothing else to learn. Knowing this, the young man moved to San Diego to continue his journey and evolve his powers with one mission in mind, to create something so beautiful, the world would stop.

...Many years have passed since that young man had begun his quest. Some say he gave up. Some say he walked until he stepped off the face of the earth. Some say he was kidnapped by an alien race to teach them of earthly things like rap music and the sport known as corn holing. Some say his powers consumed him and he went crazy.

Well, I'm here to say that he's still here, and he's still on his journey. There were some obstacles along the way, some of those obstacles almost crippled him, but now residing in northern Virginia he continues to walk, discovering new ways to use his powers. So, if you would like to see how he's been doing on his journey, take your time and have a look through this collection from his quest as Pete Tapang continues his mission to create the greatest work of all time!

*- Pete Tapang - June 2013,*

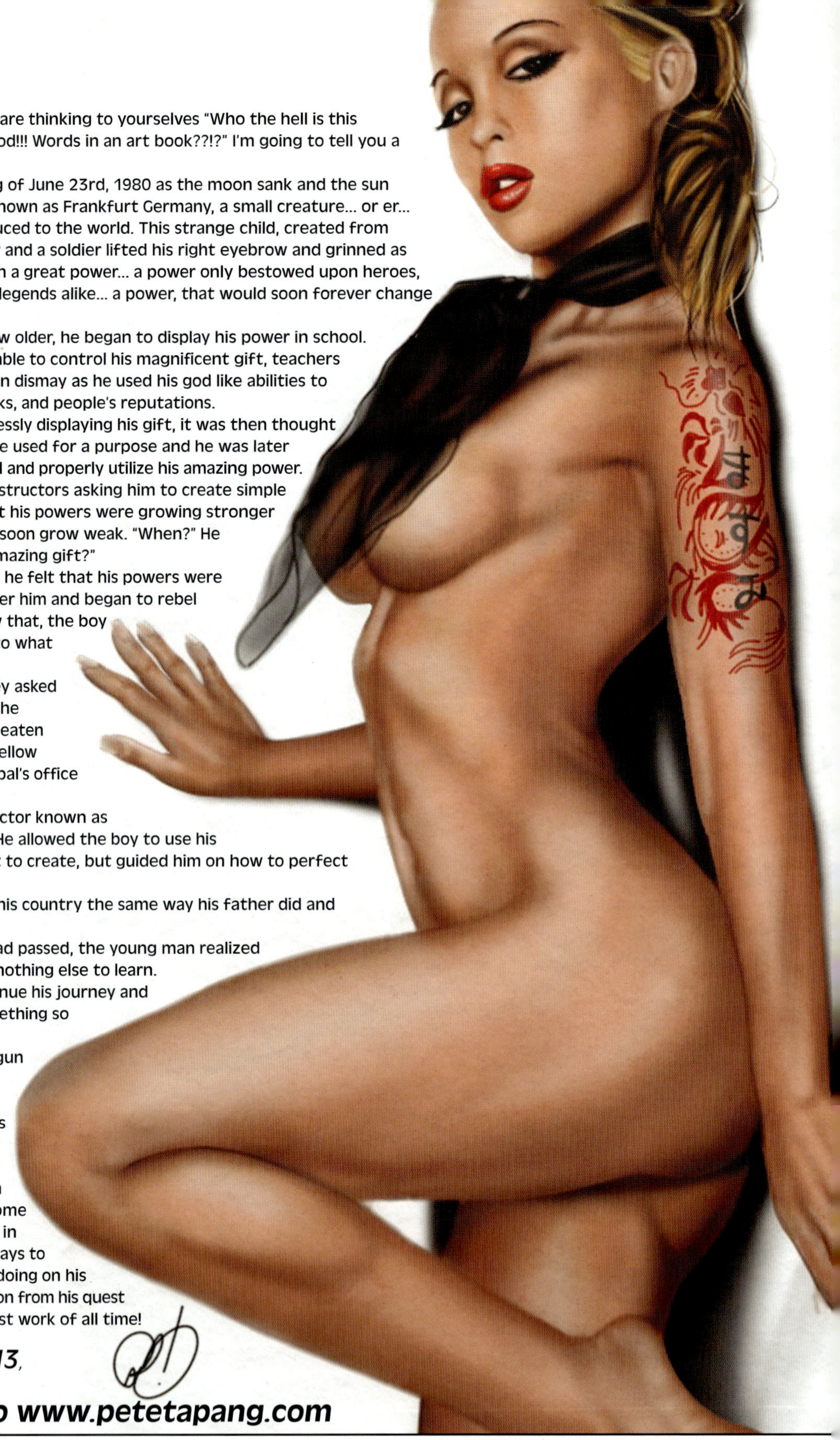

***For the latest on Mr Tapang go to www.petetapang.com***

## The Art of Pete Tapang



Book design by Grassy Knoll Studios.

Published by SQP Inc.
PO Box 248 - Columbus NJ 08022

Sal Quartuccio & Bob Keenan - Publishers

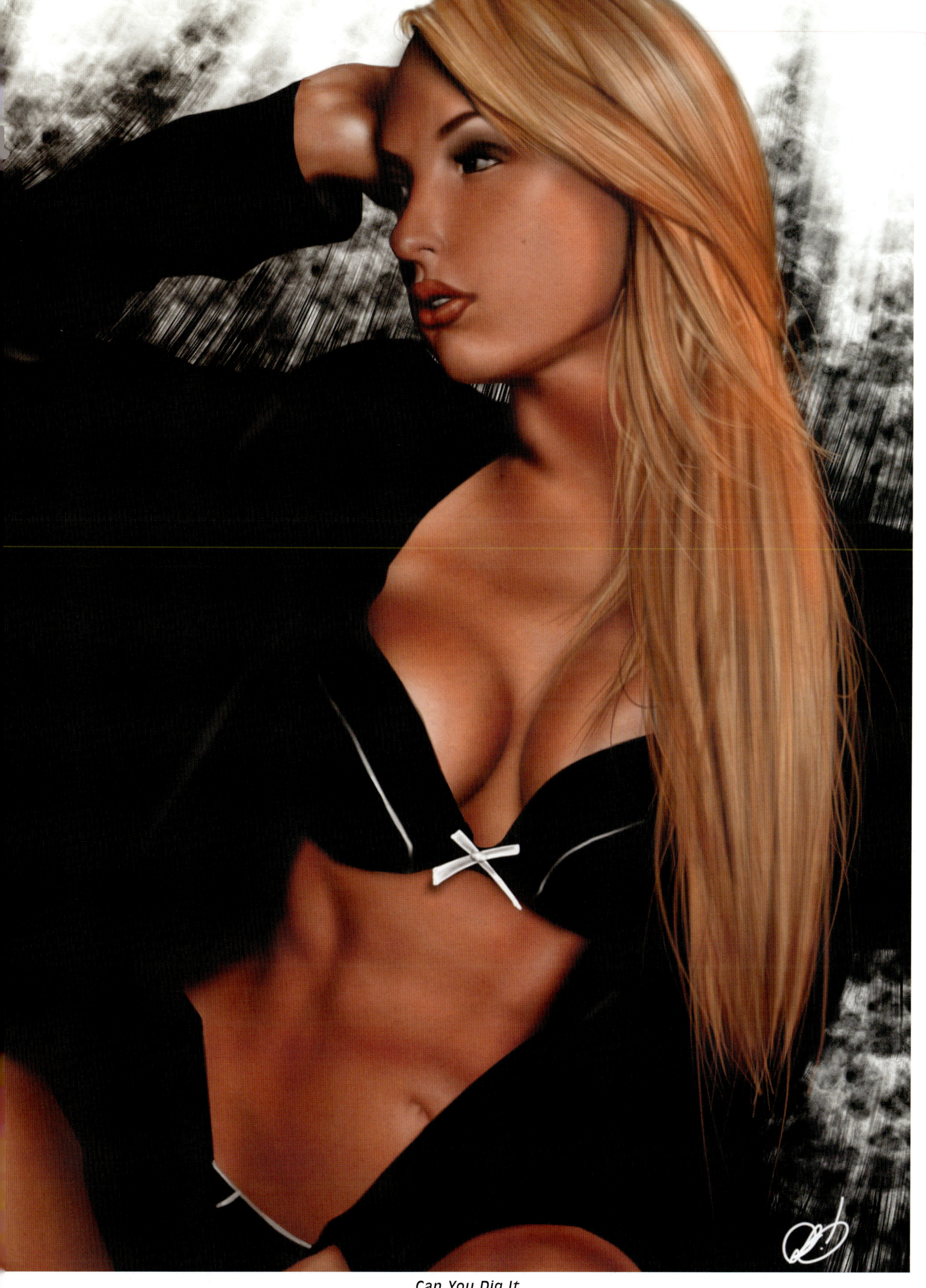

*Can You Dig It*

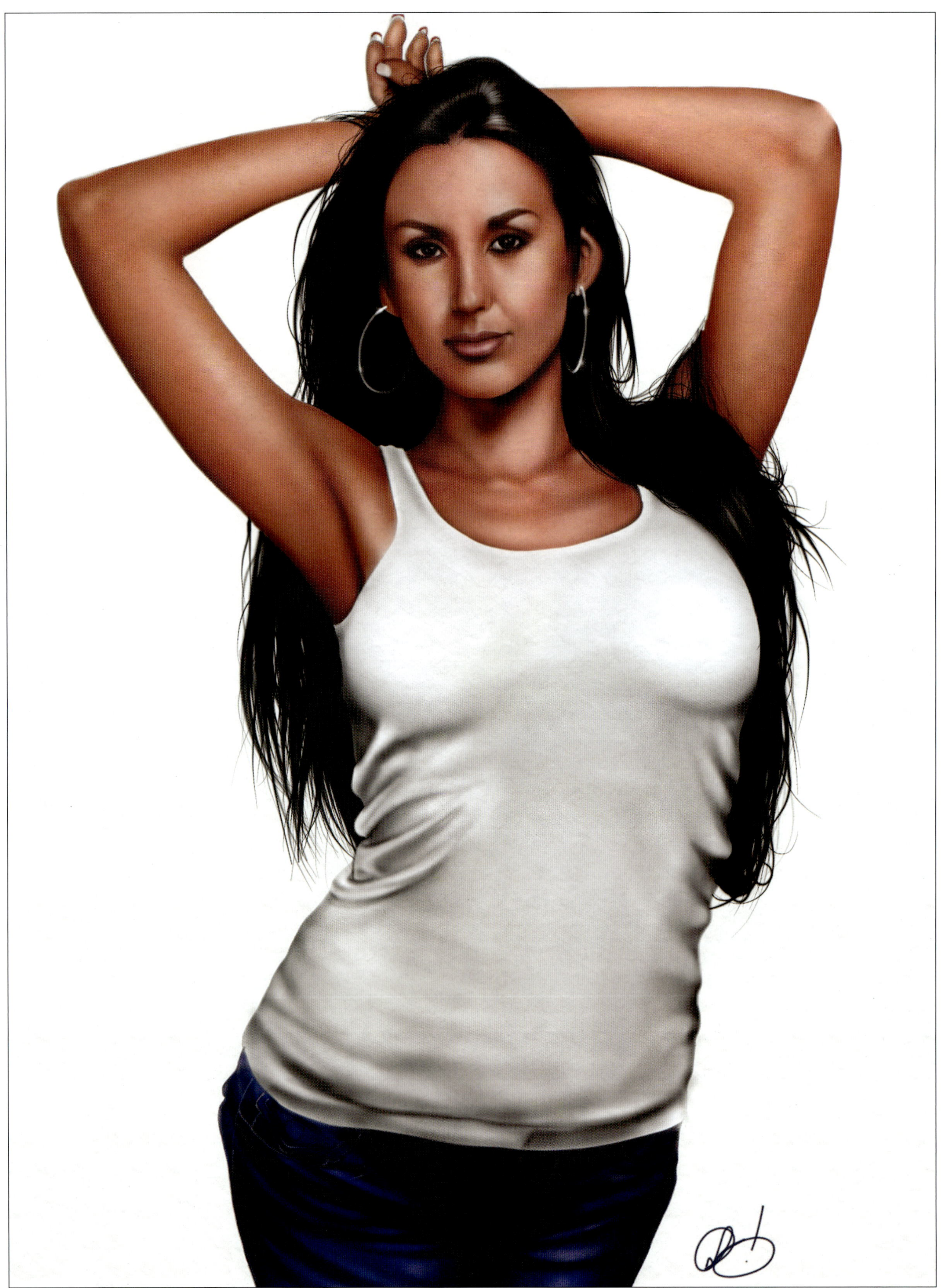

*Vanity*

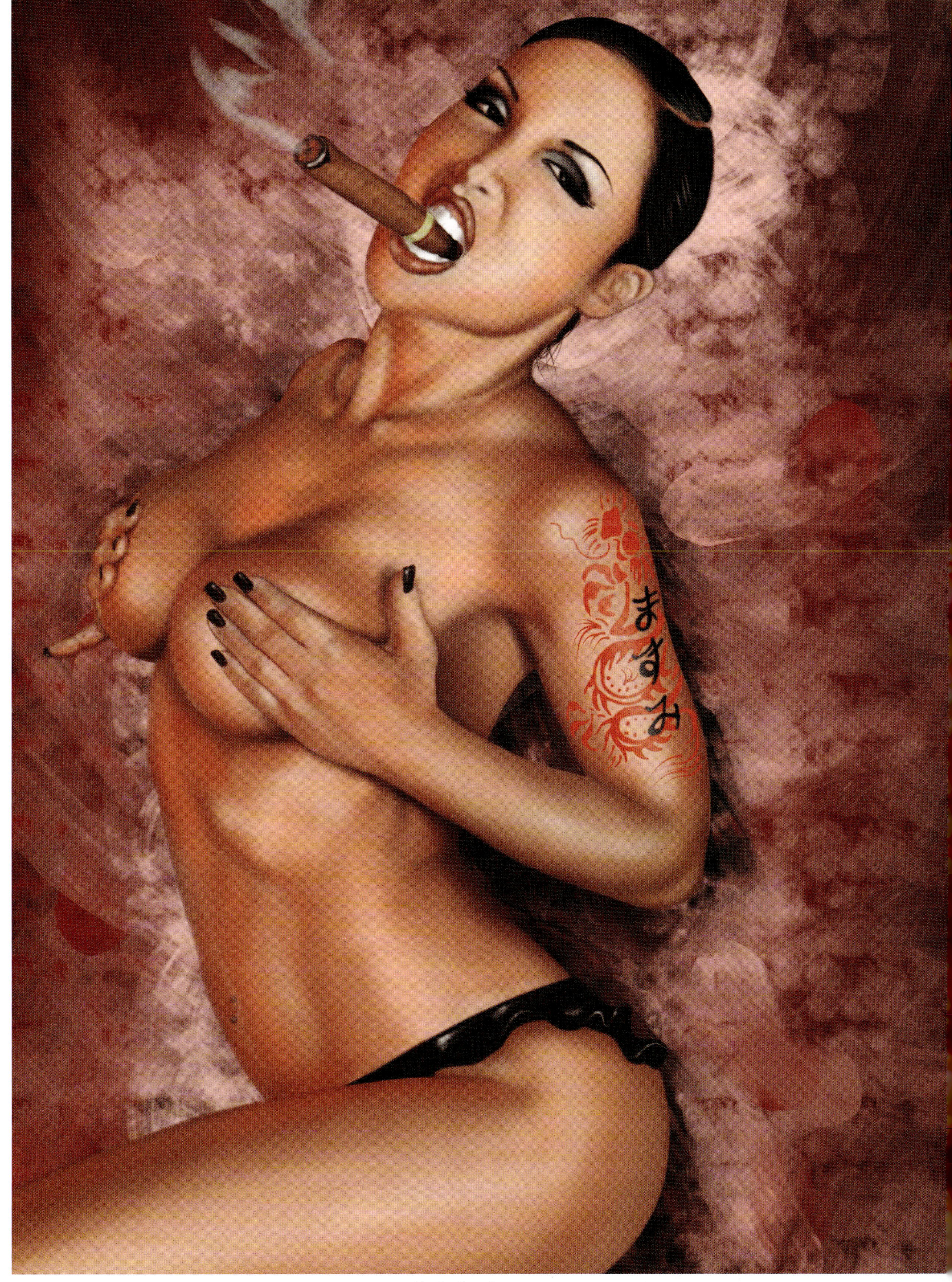


*Up In Smoke*

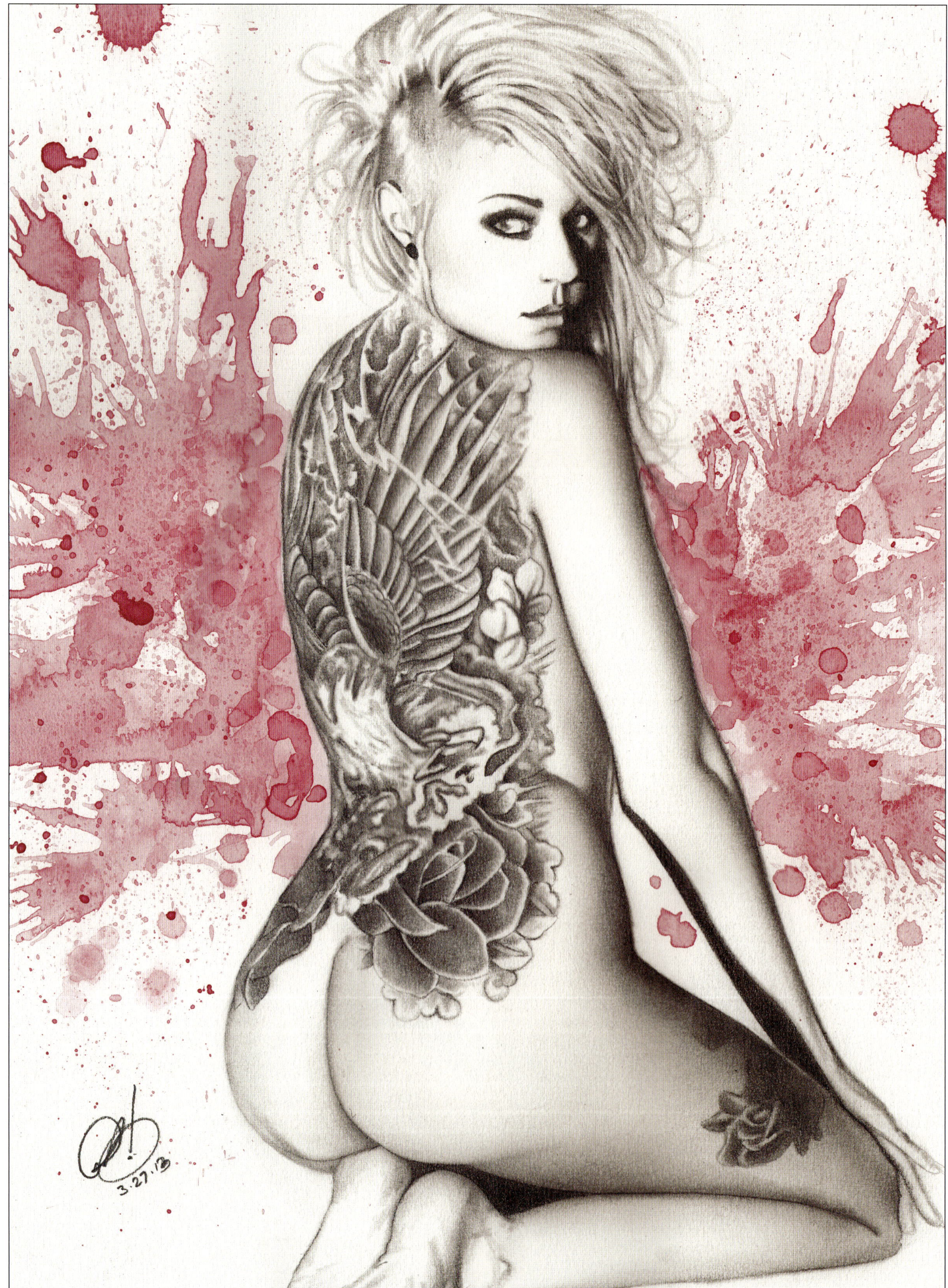


*Purple Lake*

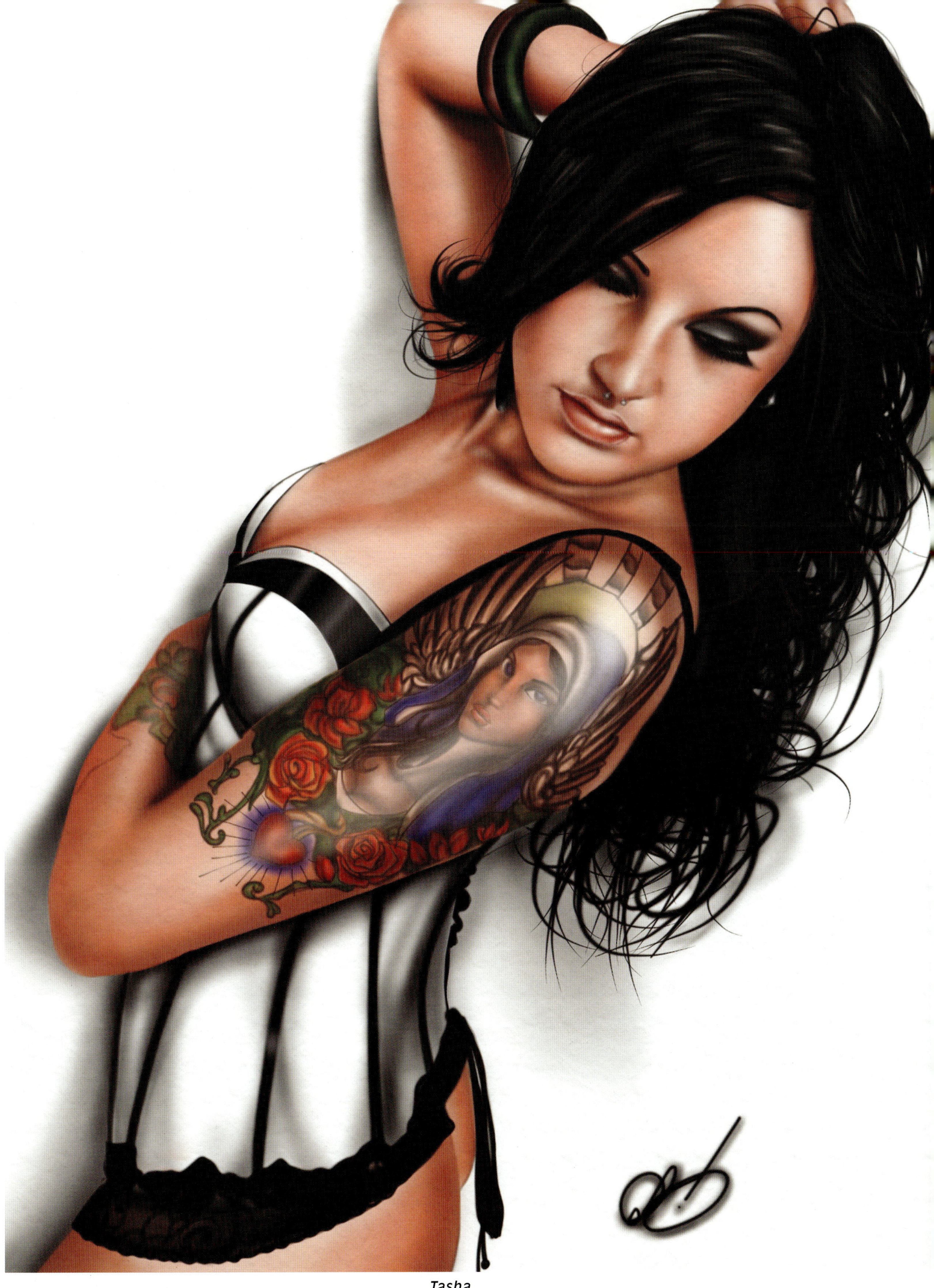

*Tasha*

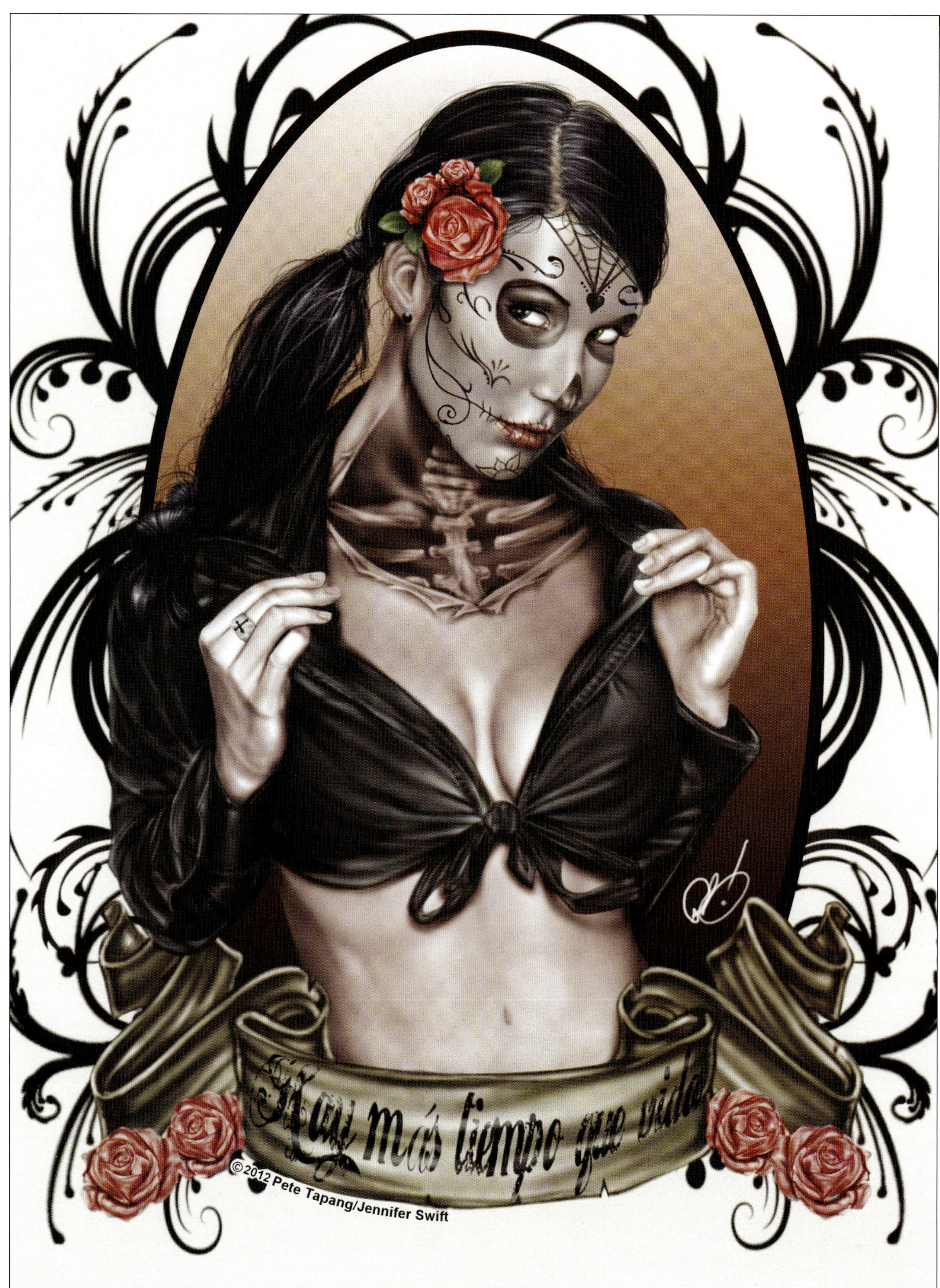


Operation Cupcake

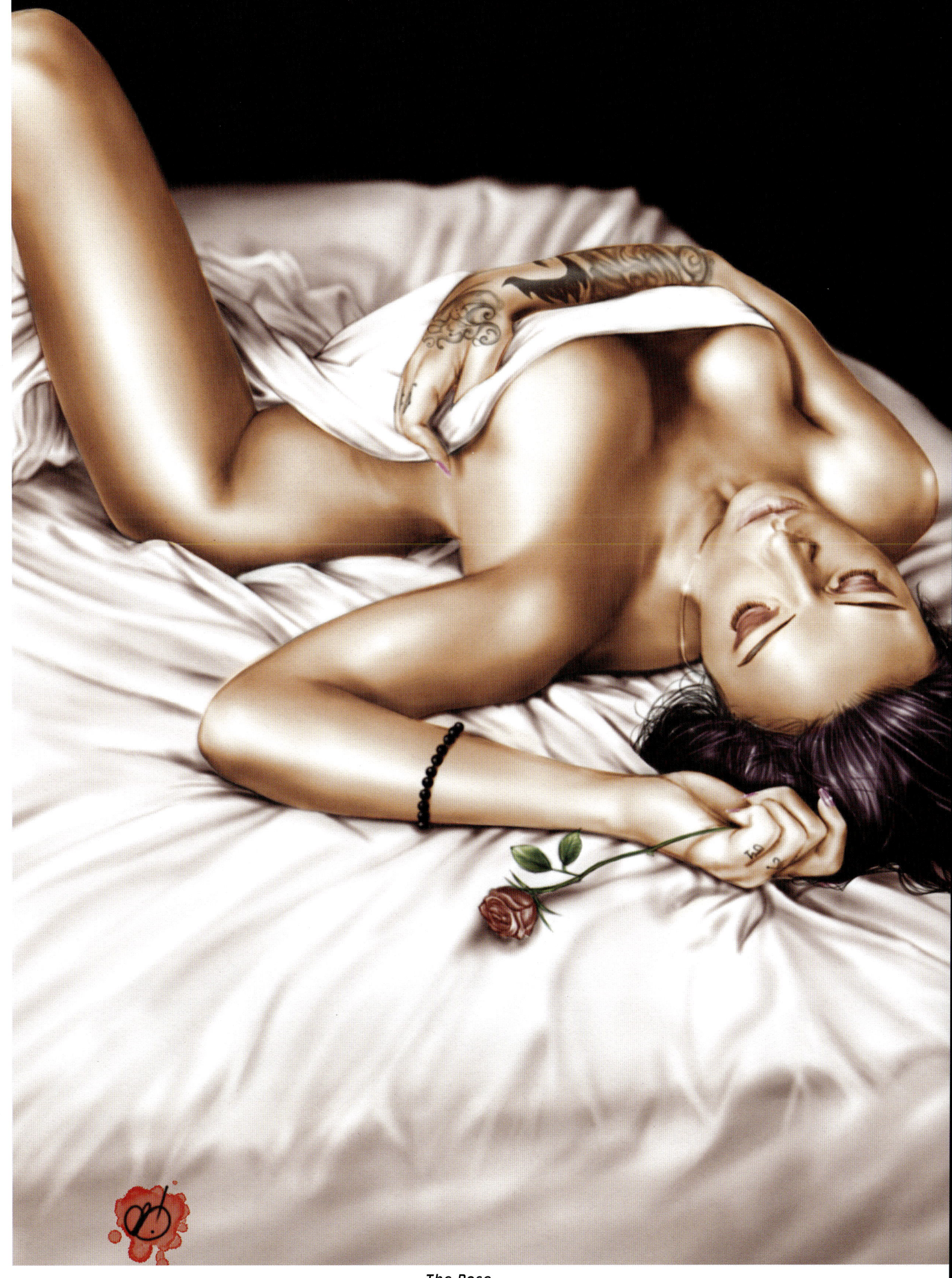

*The Rose*

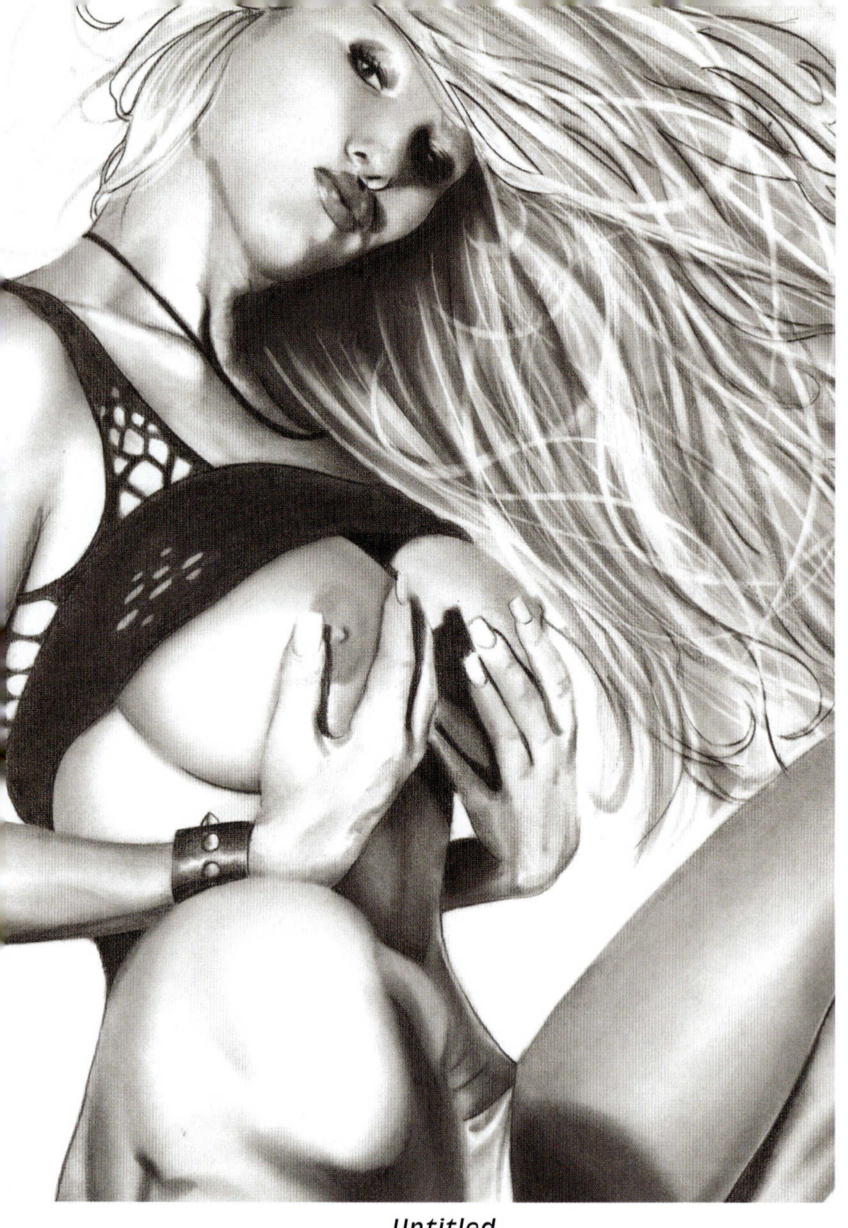

*Untitled*

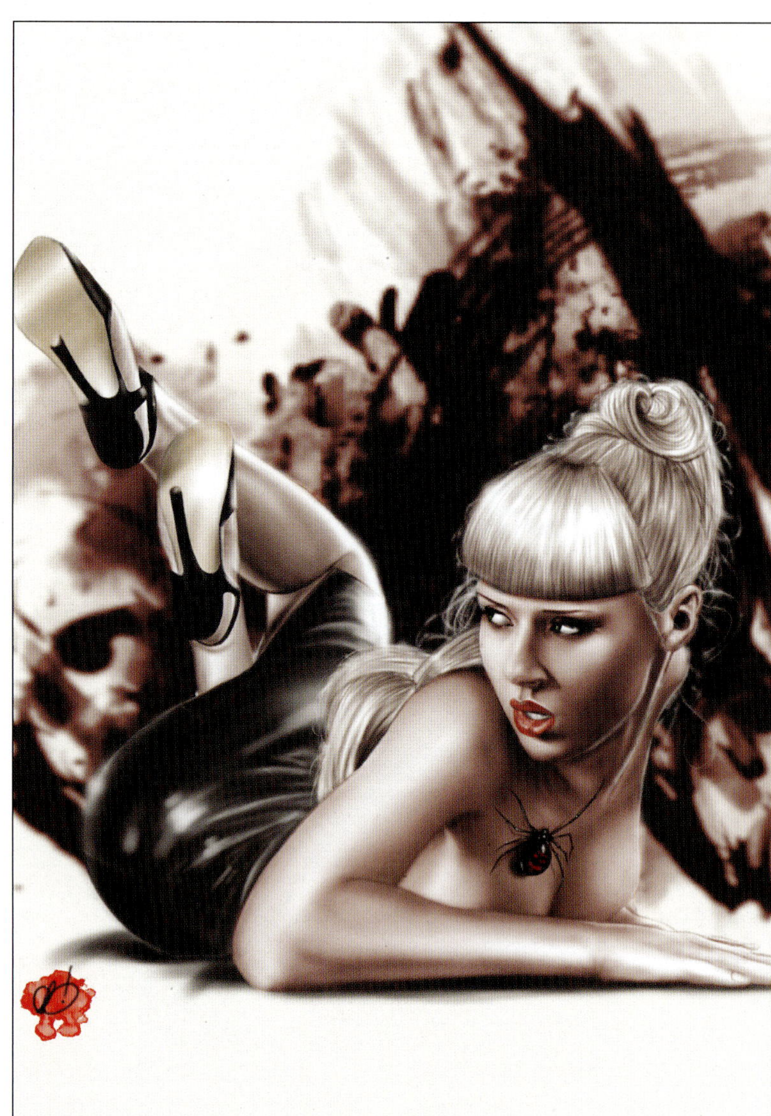

*Spider Webs*

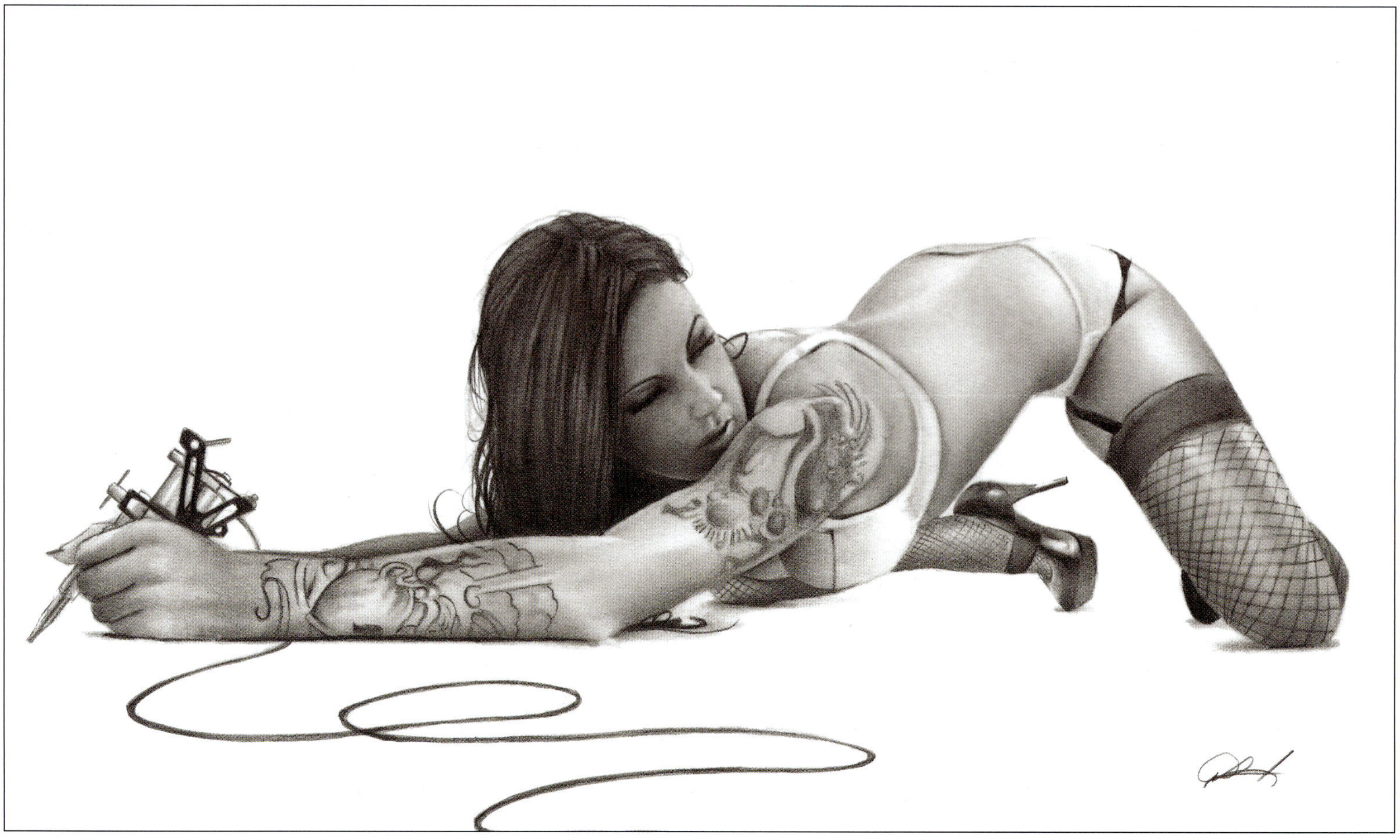

*Ink Angel*

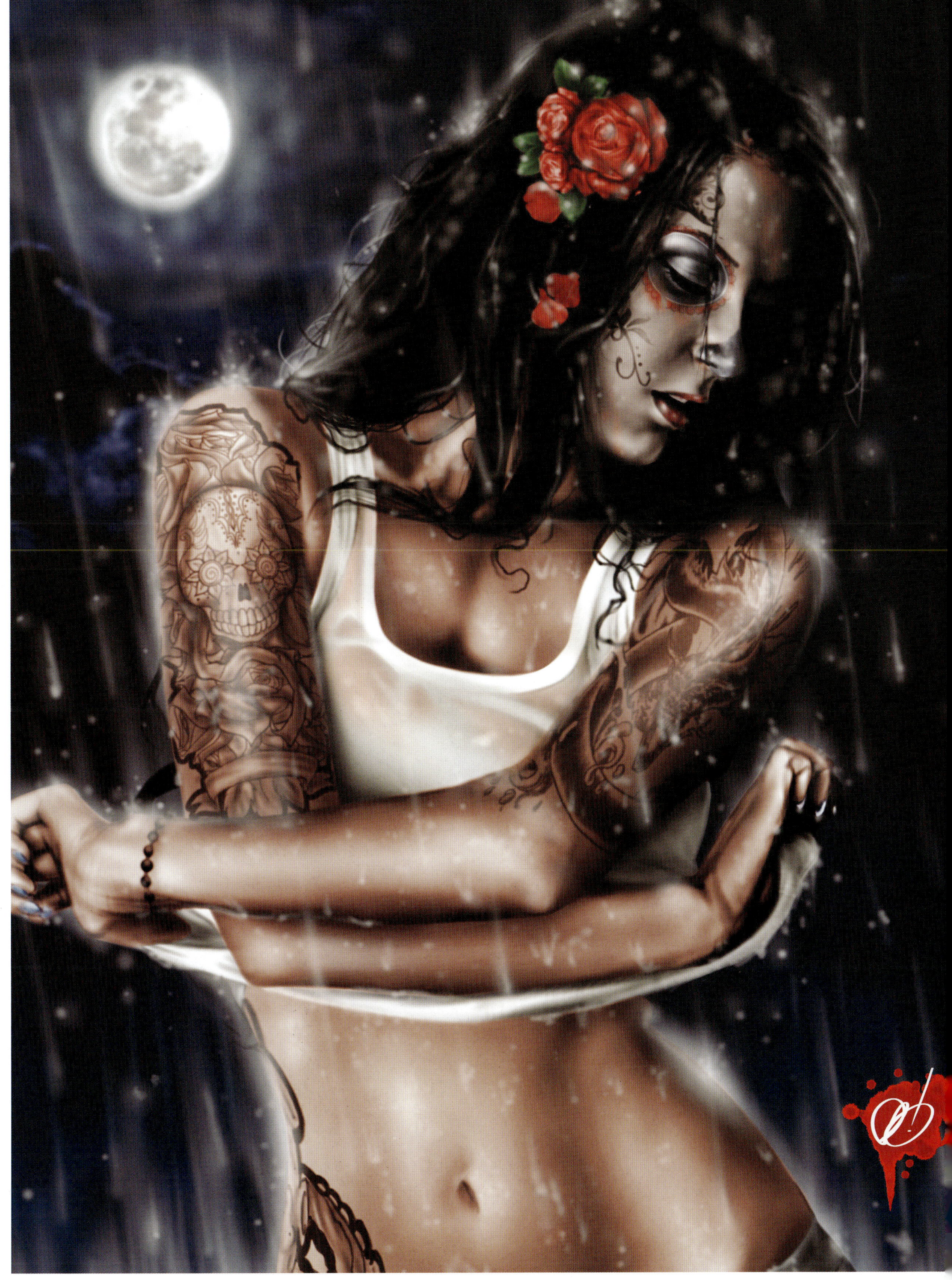

Rain When I Die

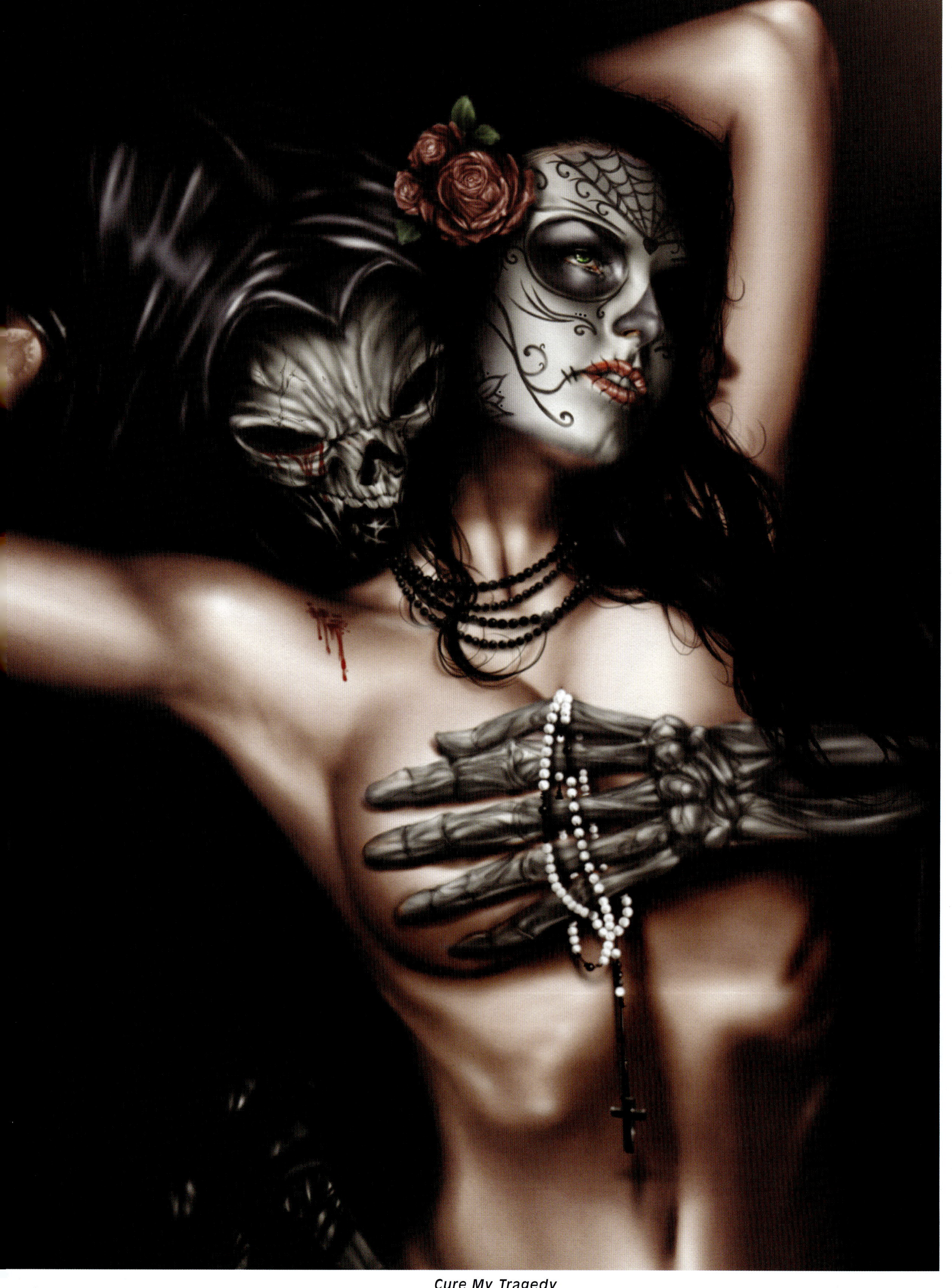

*Cure My Tragedy*

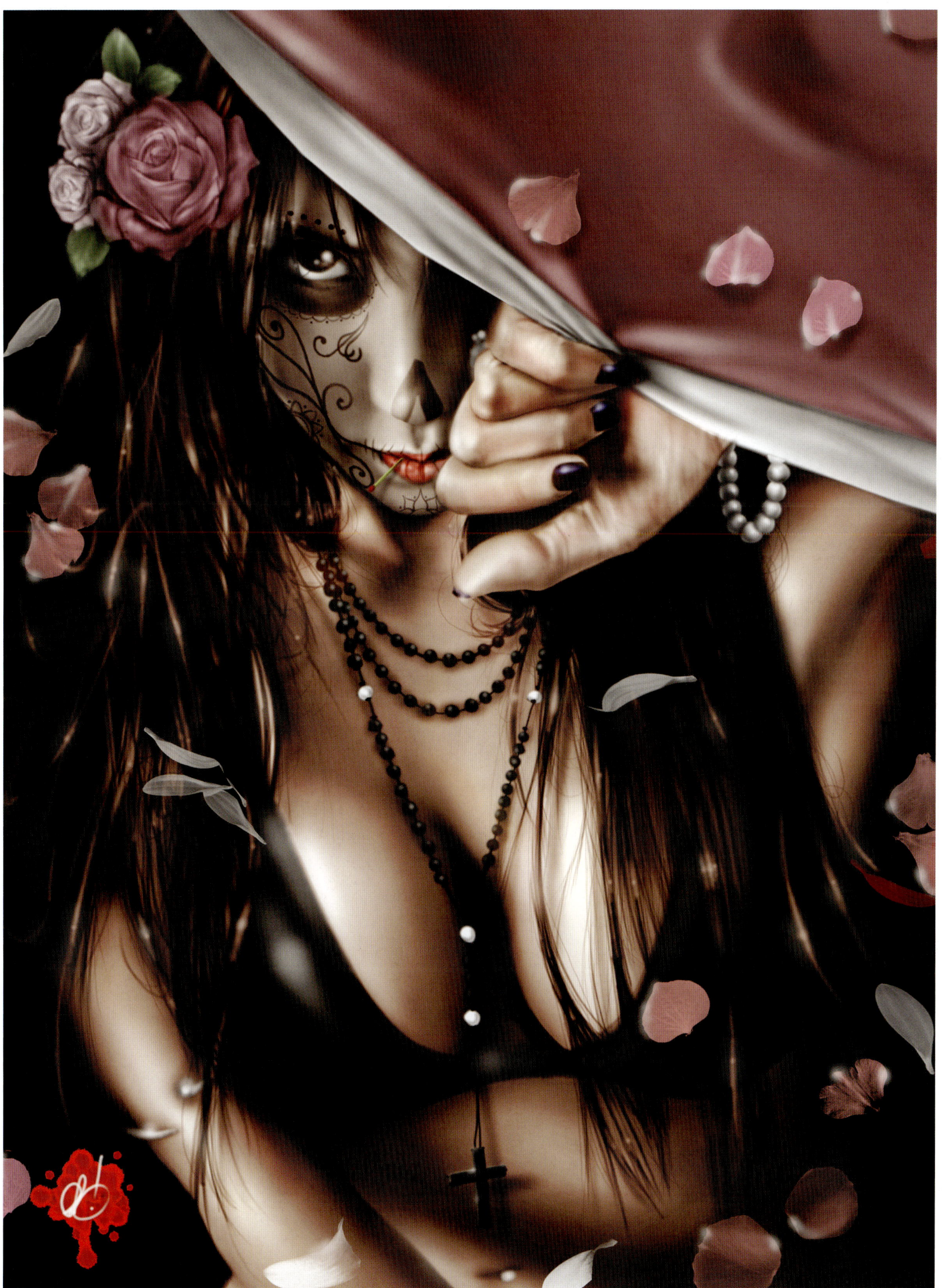

*Cemetary Gates*

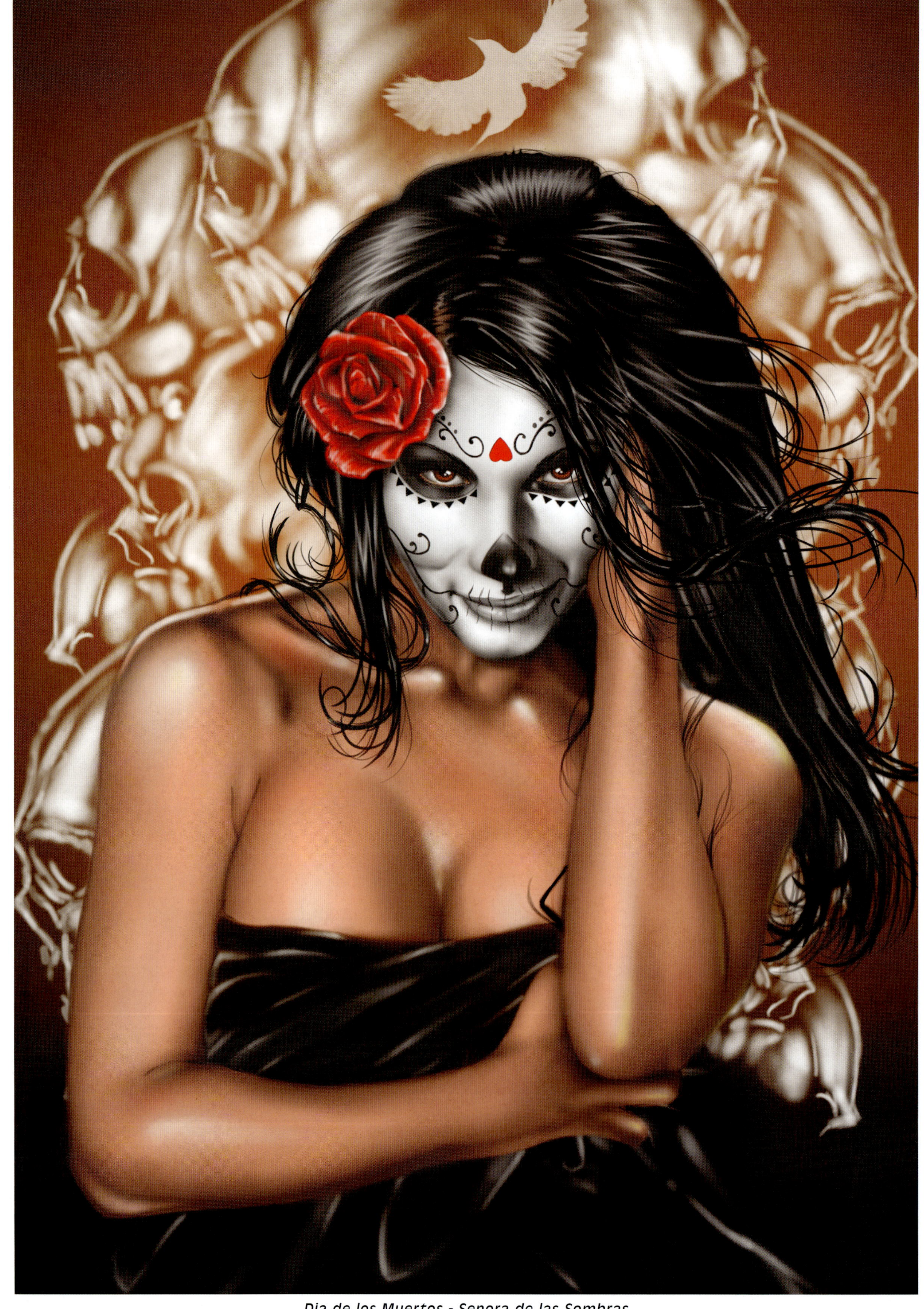

*Dia de los Muertos - Senora de las Sombras*

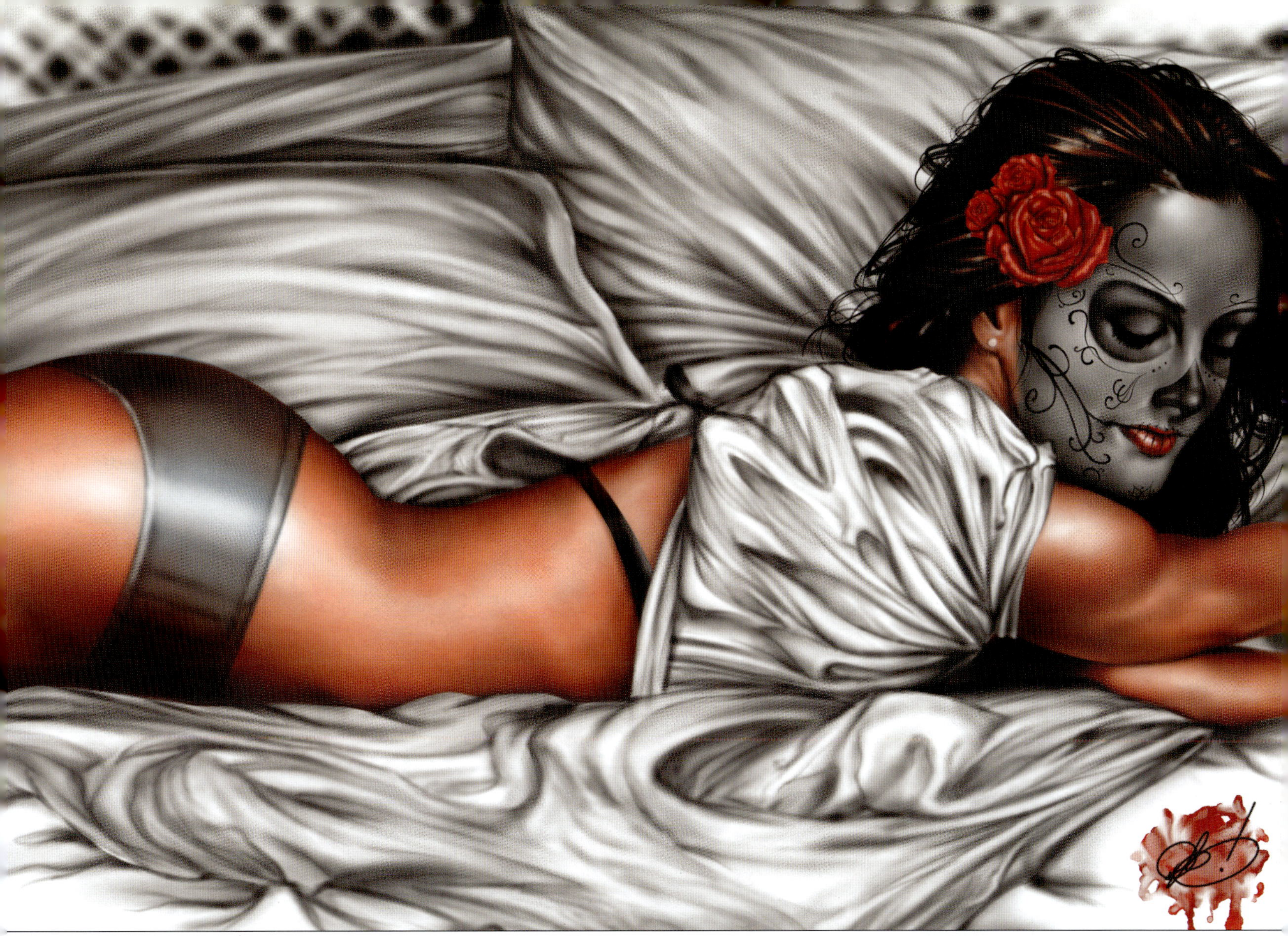

The Last Judgement

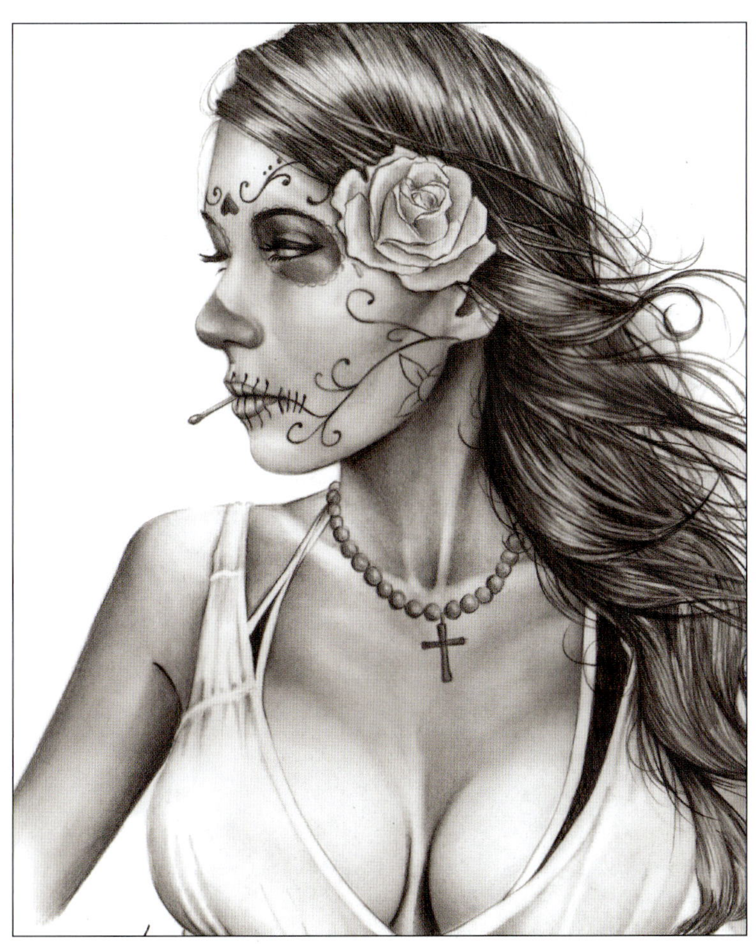

Dia de los Muertos 1

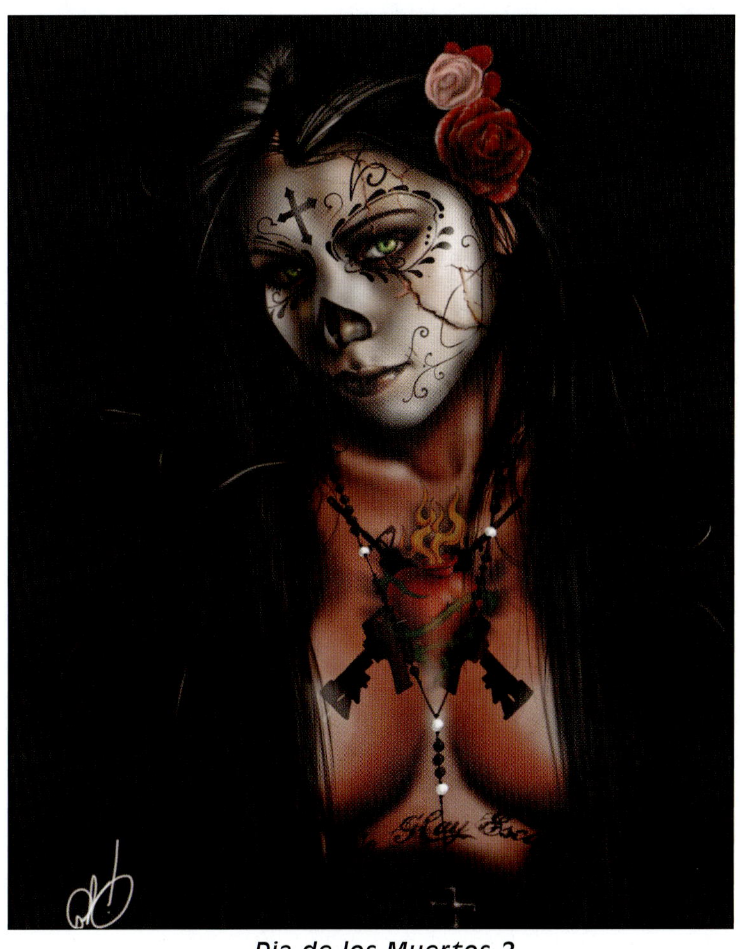

Dia de los Muertos 2

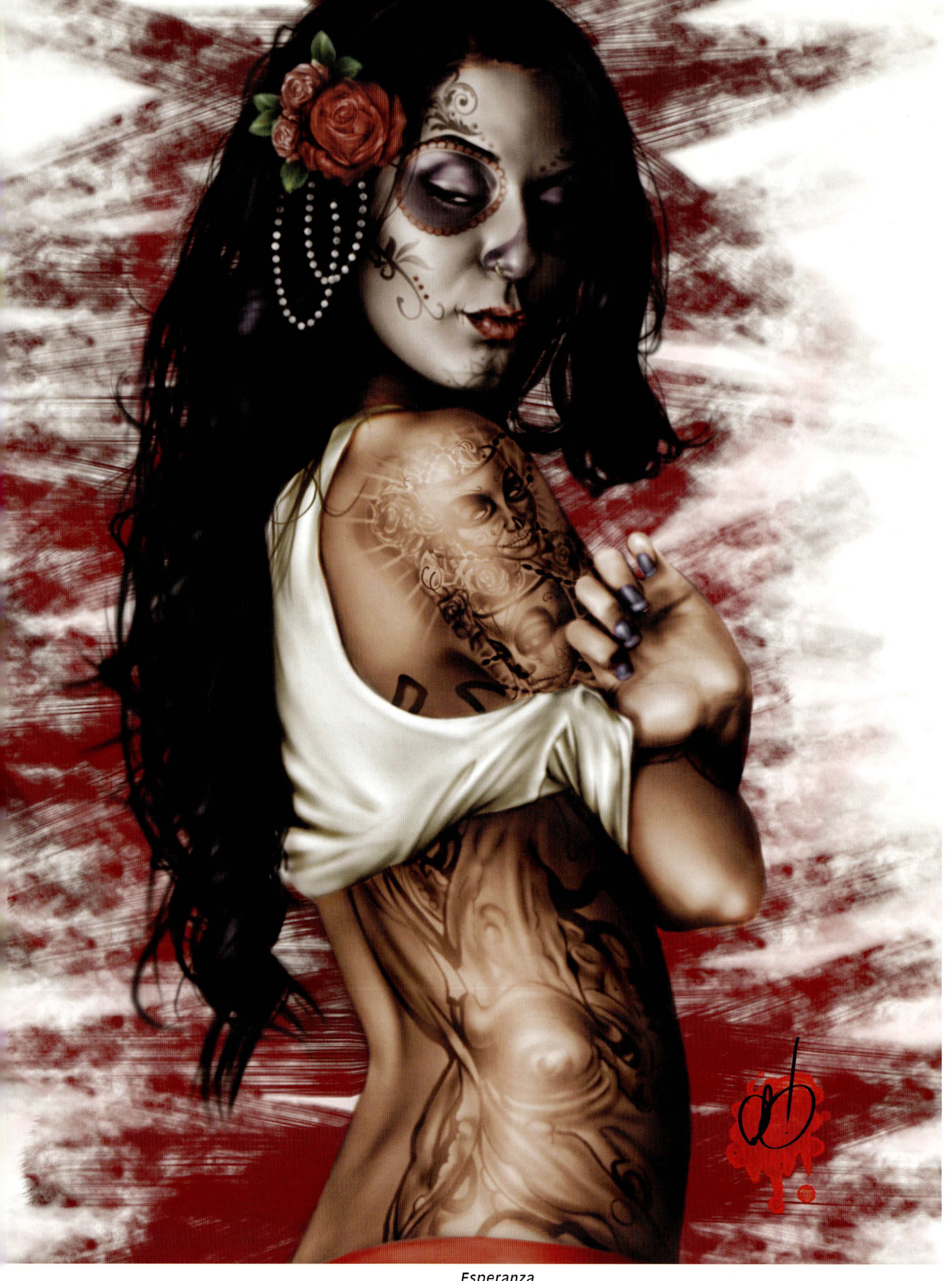

*Esperanza*

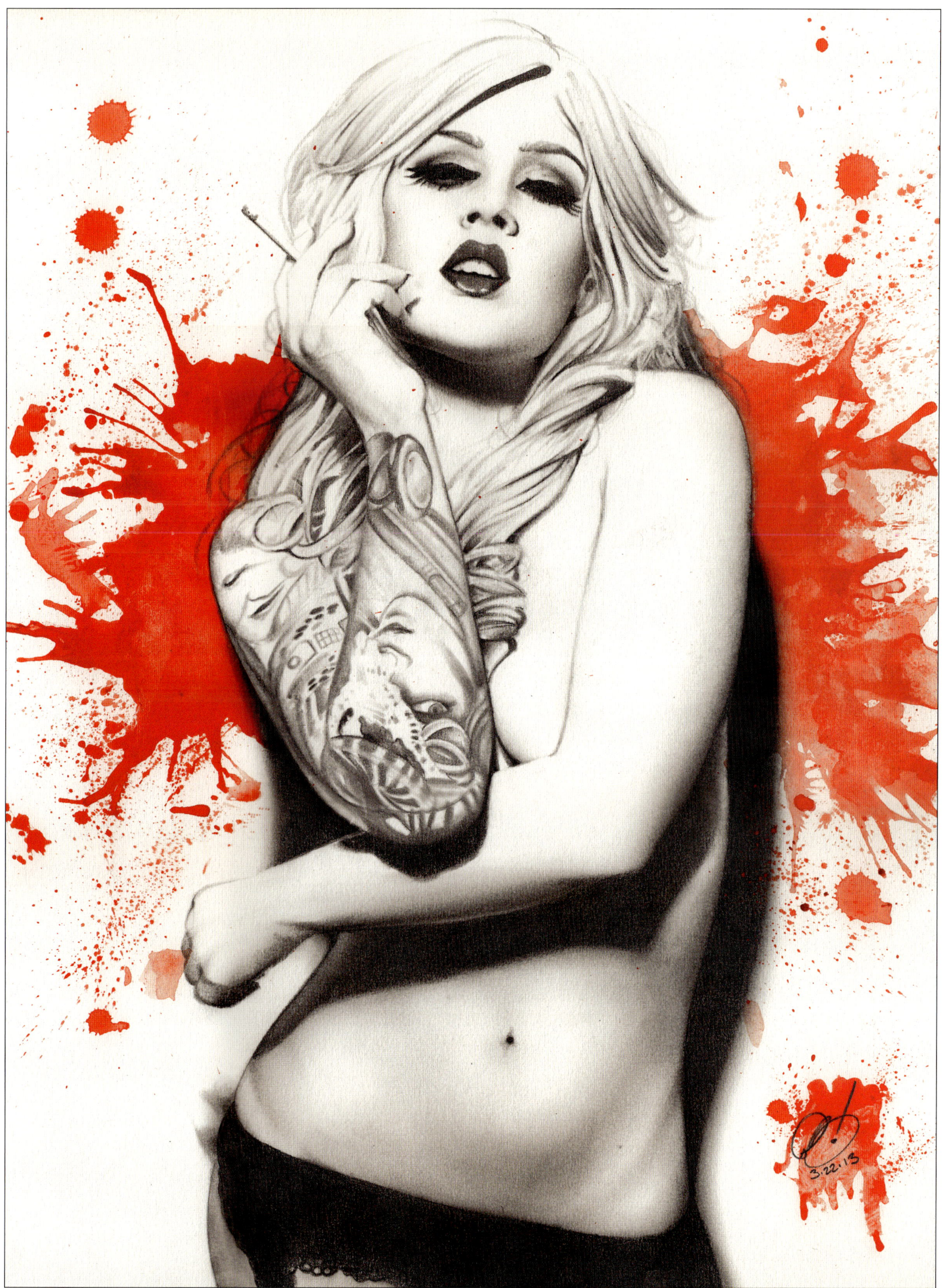

*Vermillion*

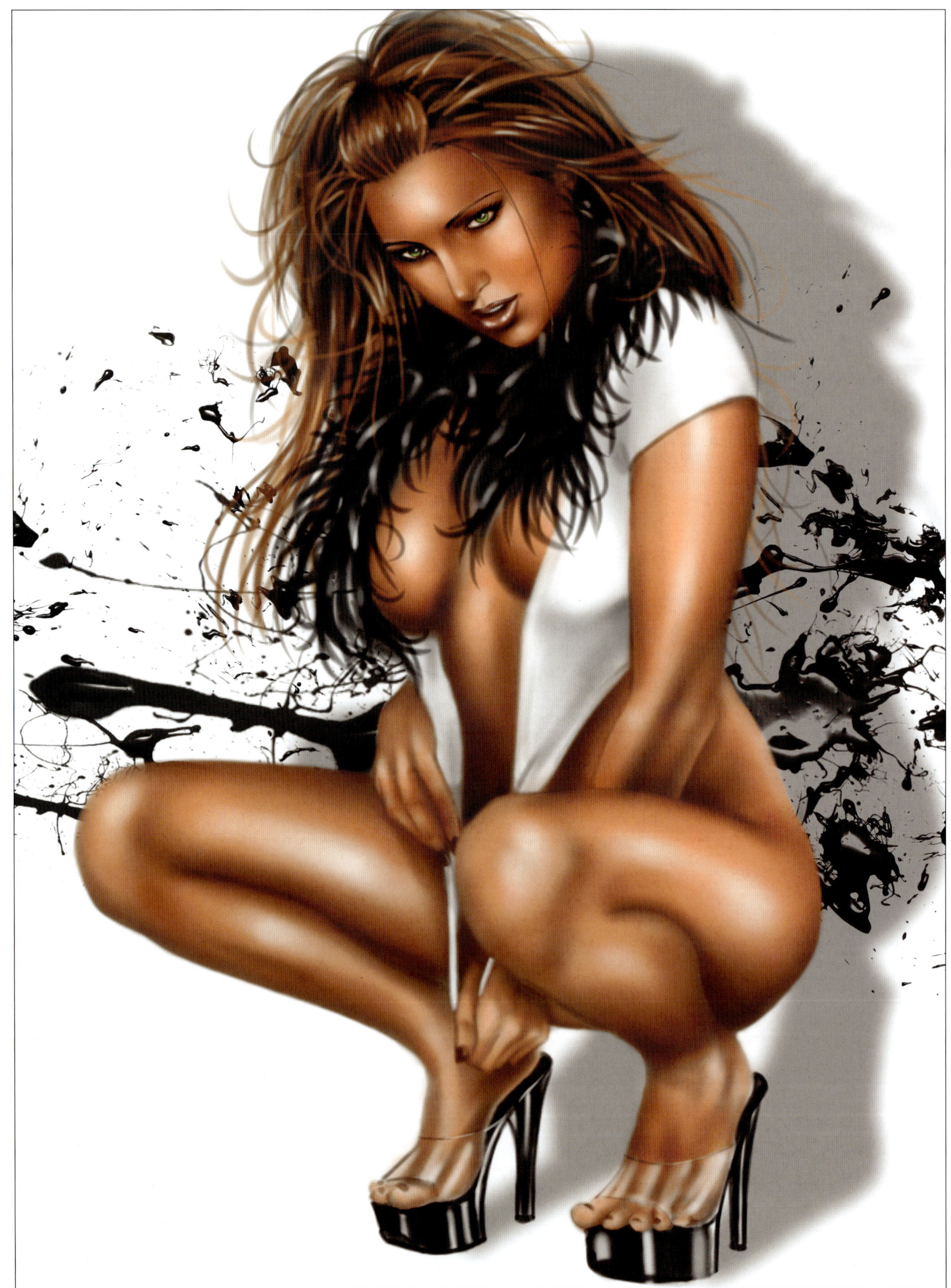

*Gray Fox*

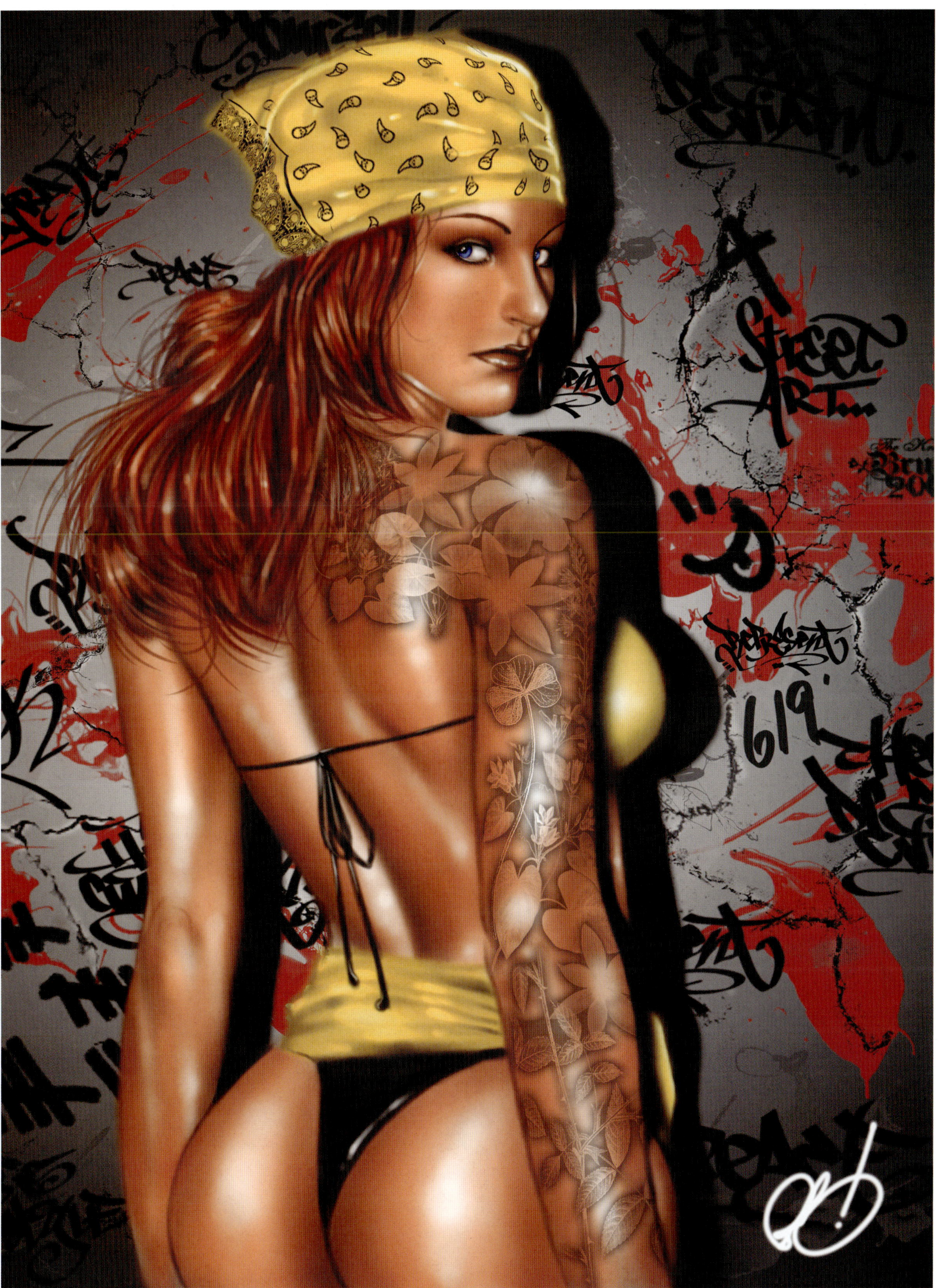


Silver

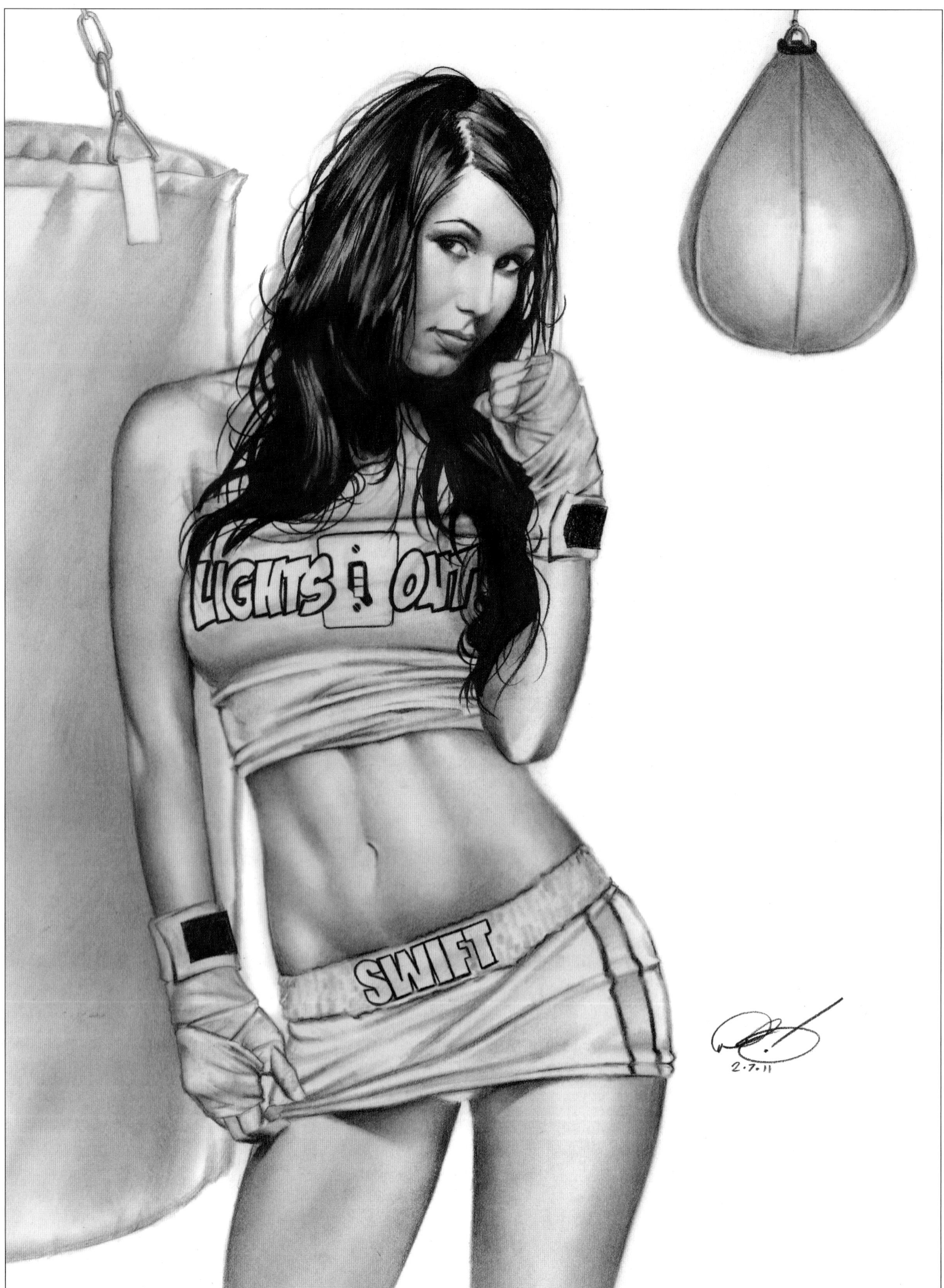


*Lights Out 1*

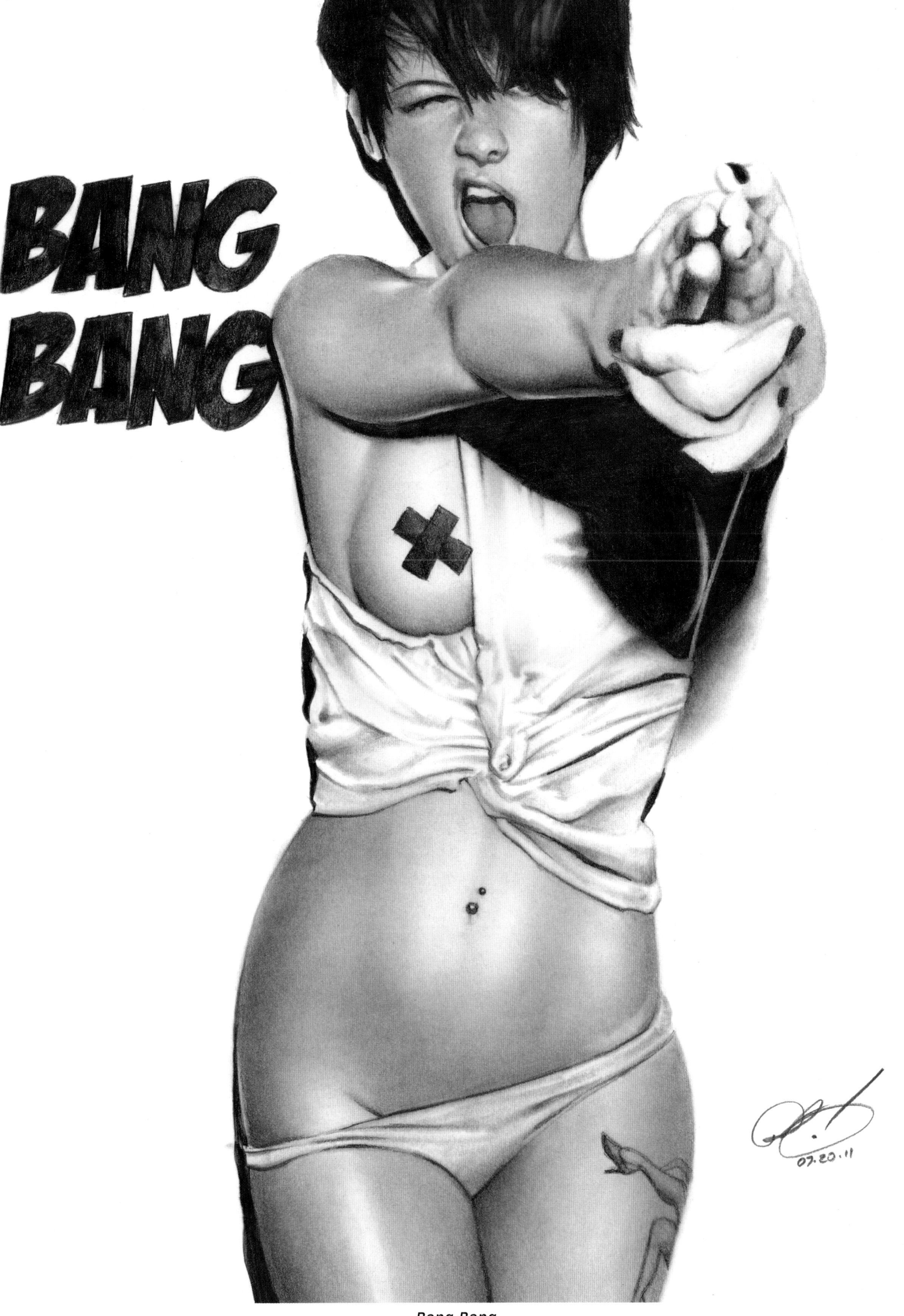


*Bang Bang*

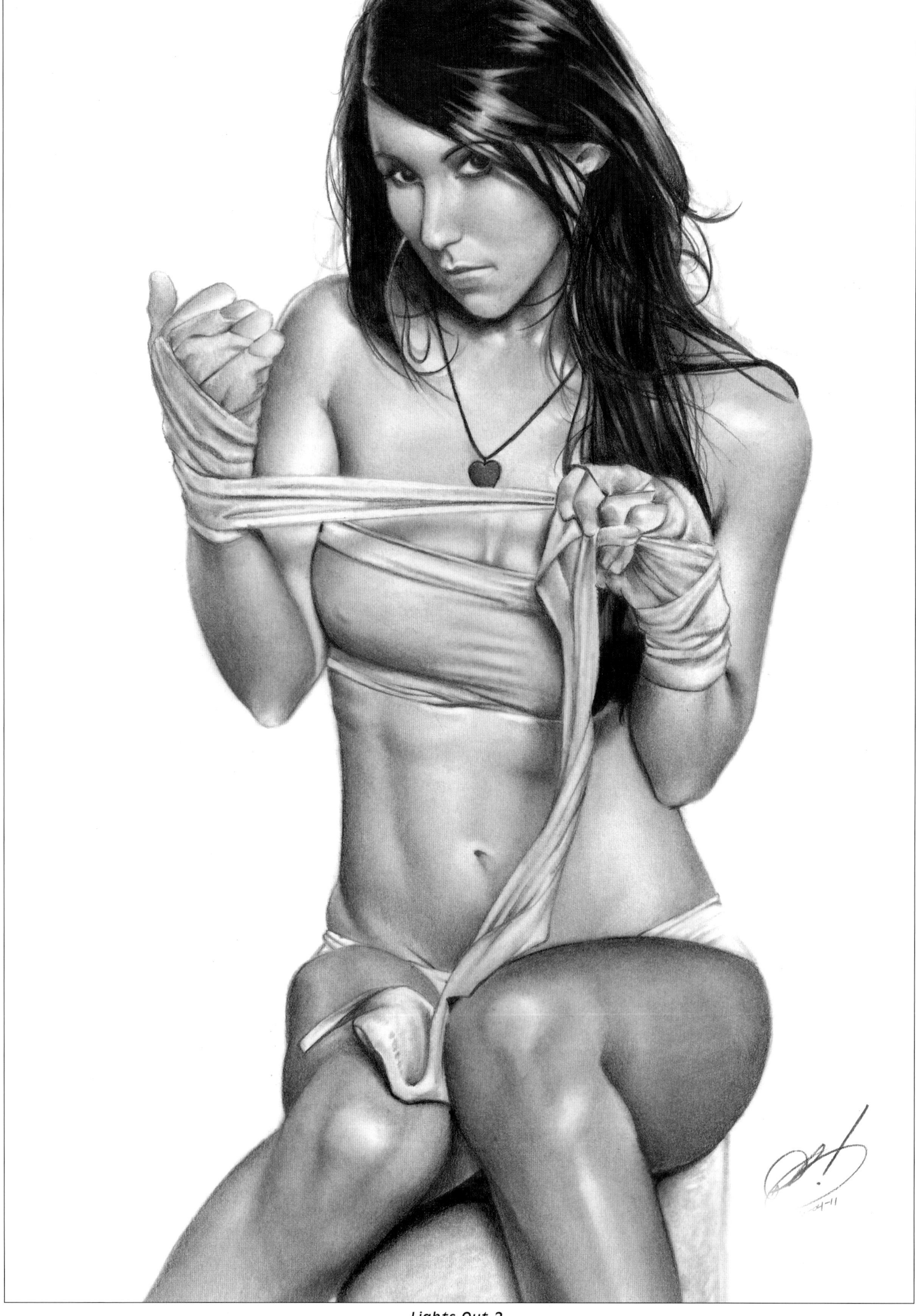

*Lights Out 2*

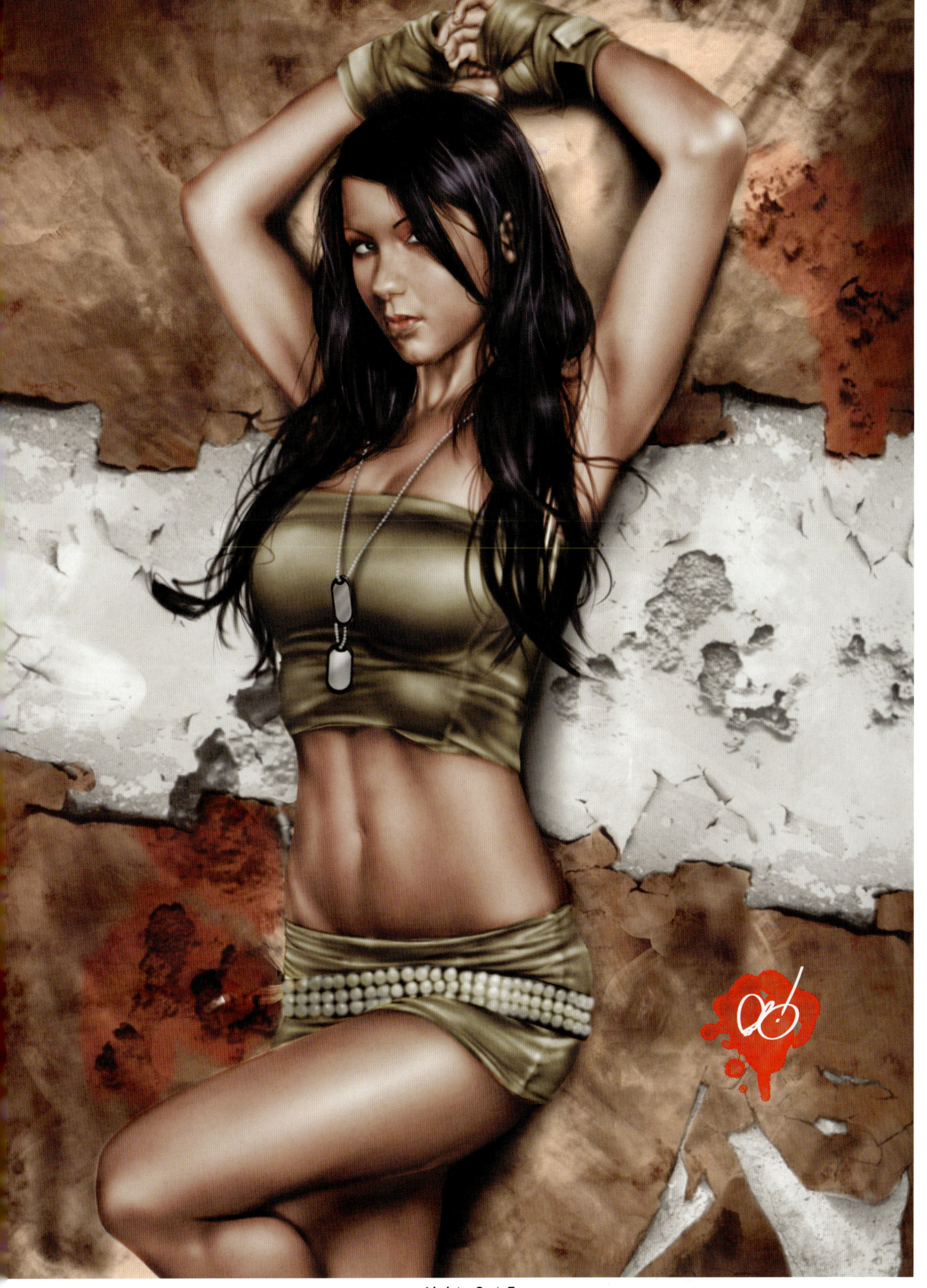

*Lights Out 3*

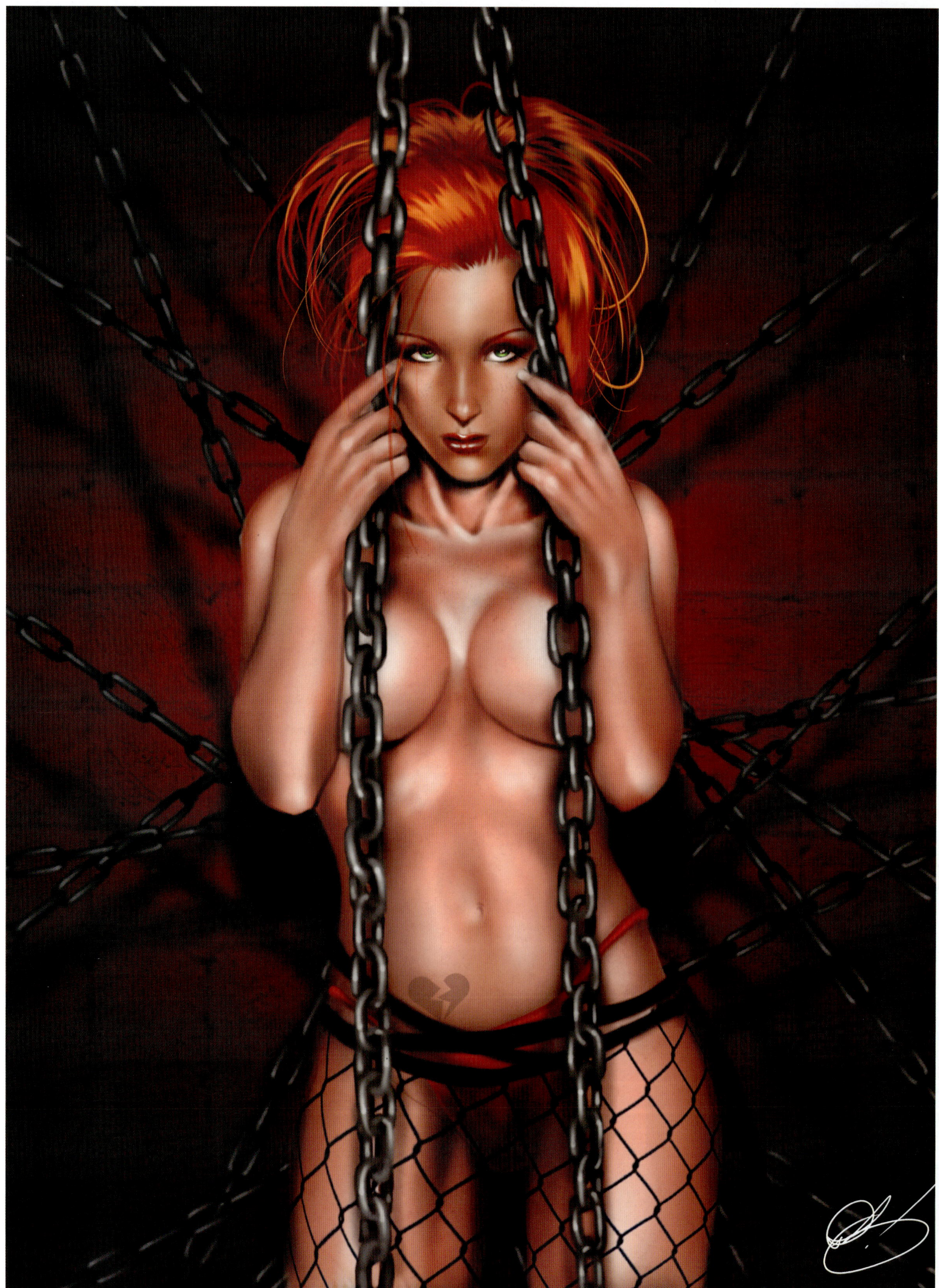

Chains Remix

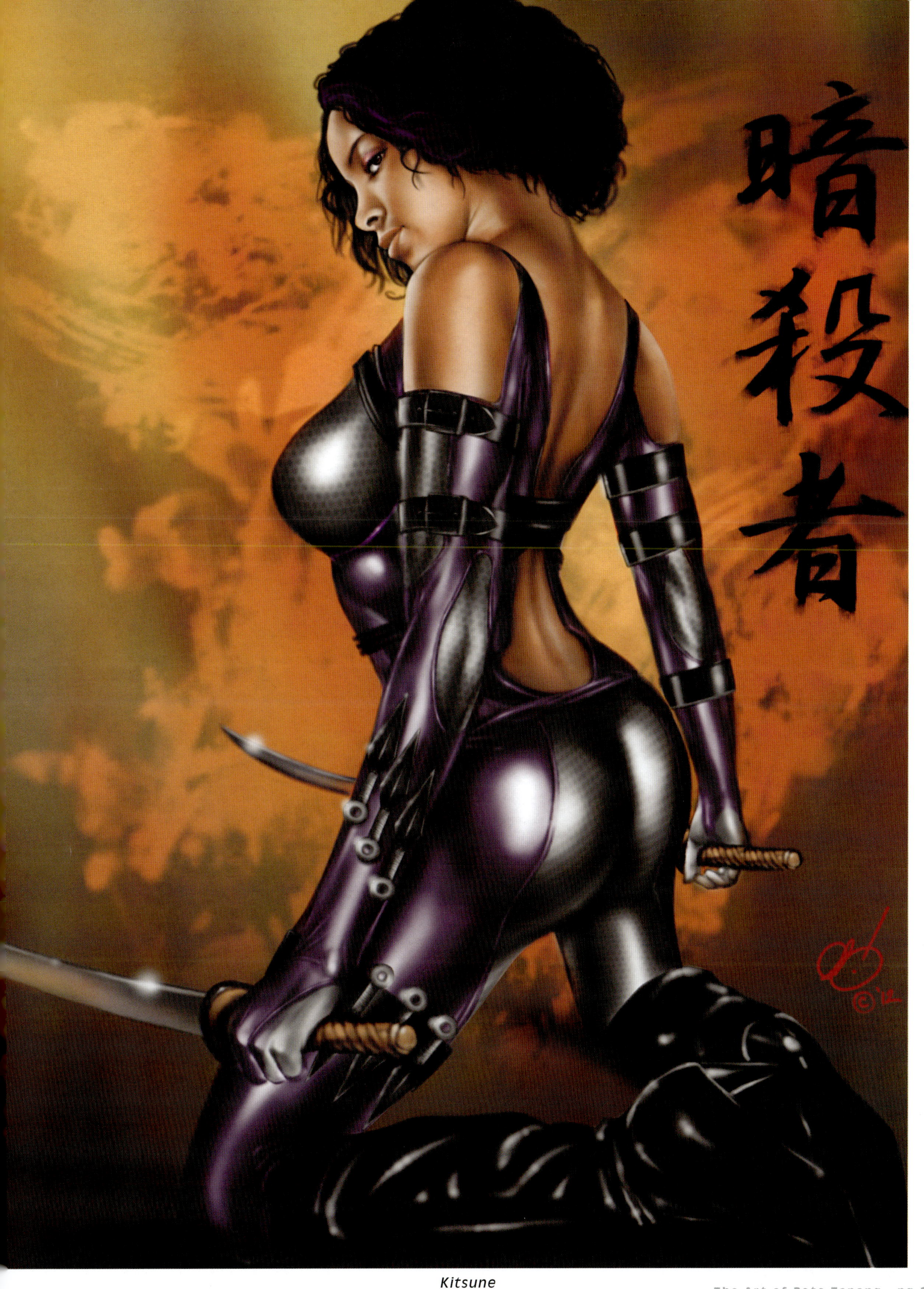


*Kitsune*

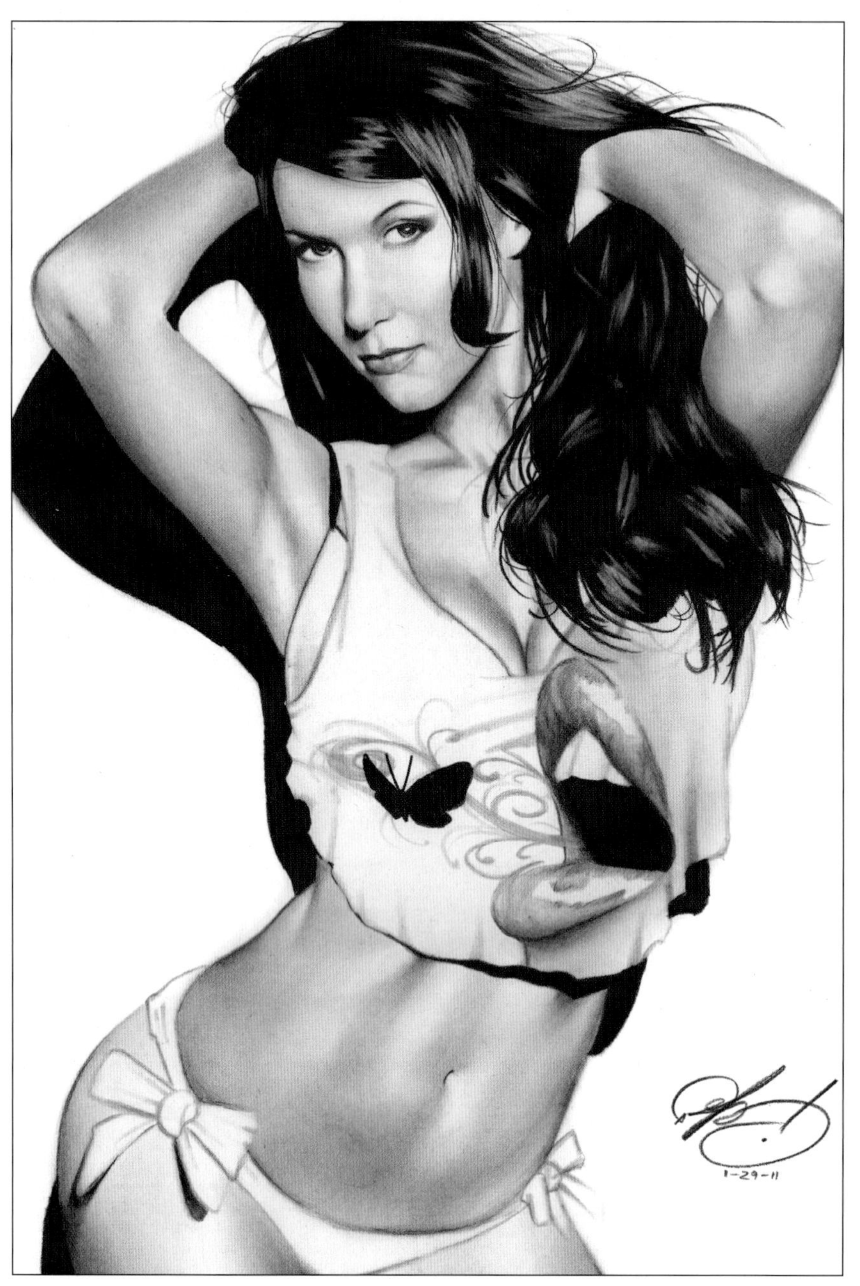


*Whispers*

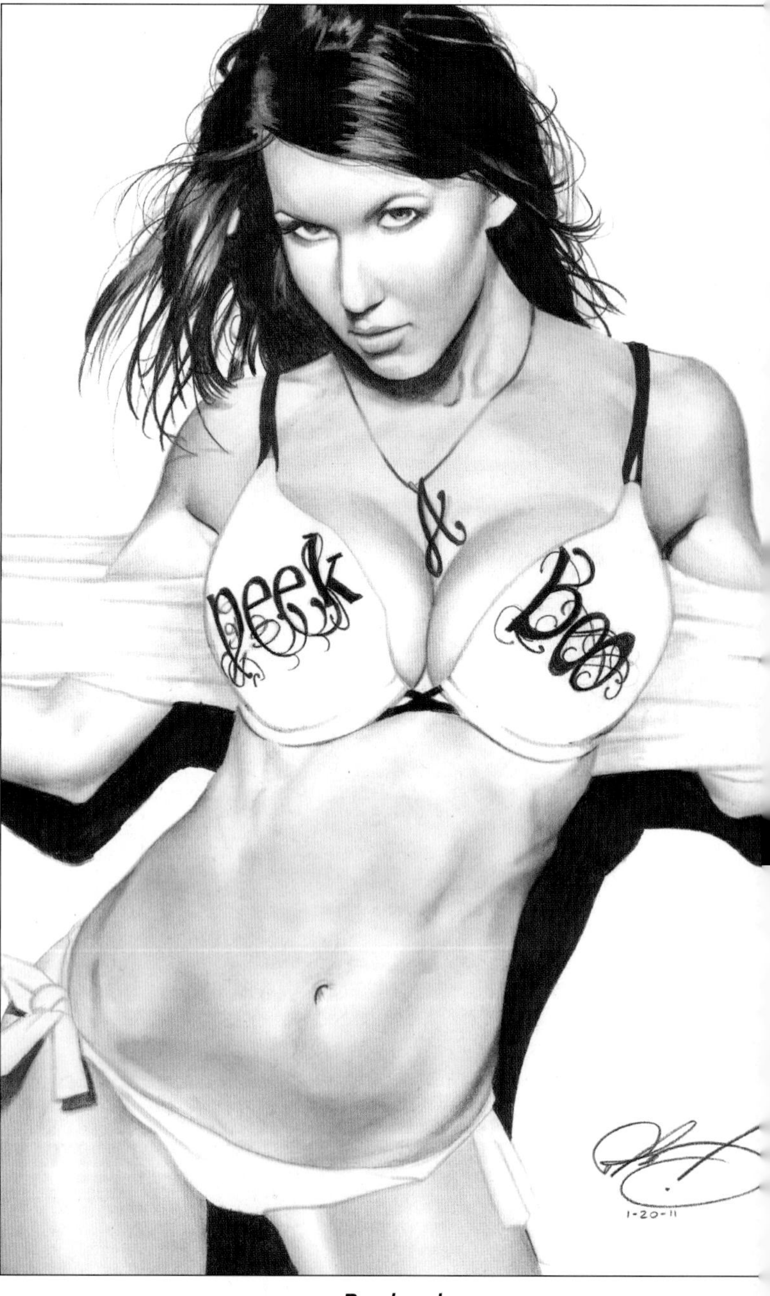


*Peek-a-boo*

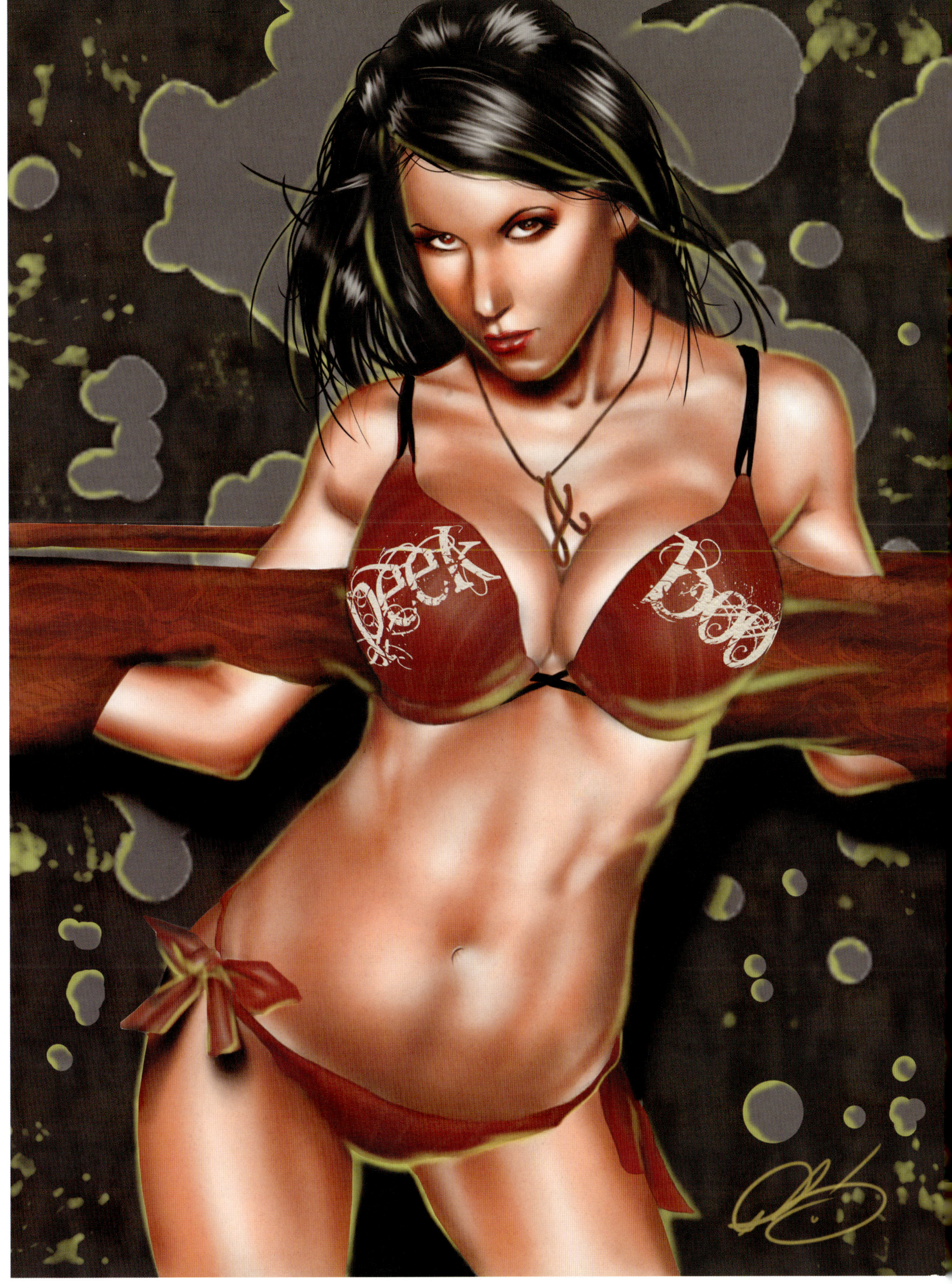

*Peek-a-boo Remix*

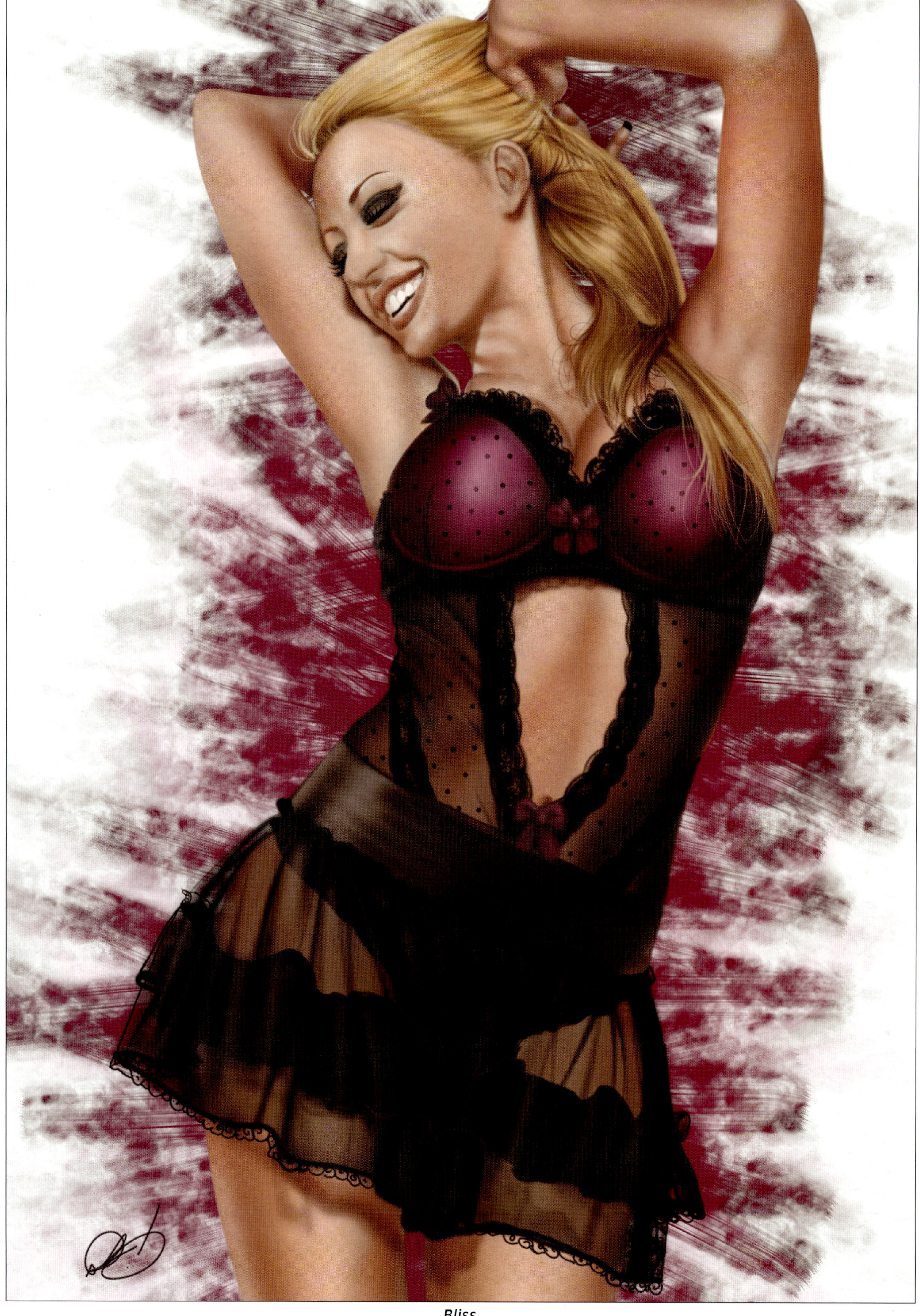

*Bliss*

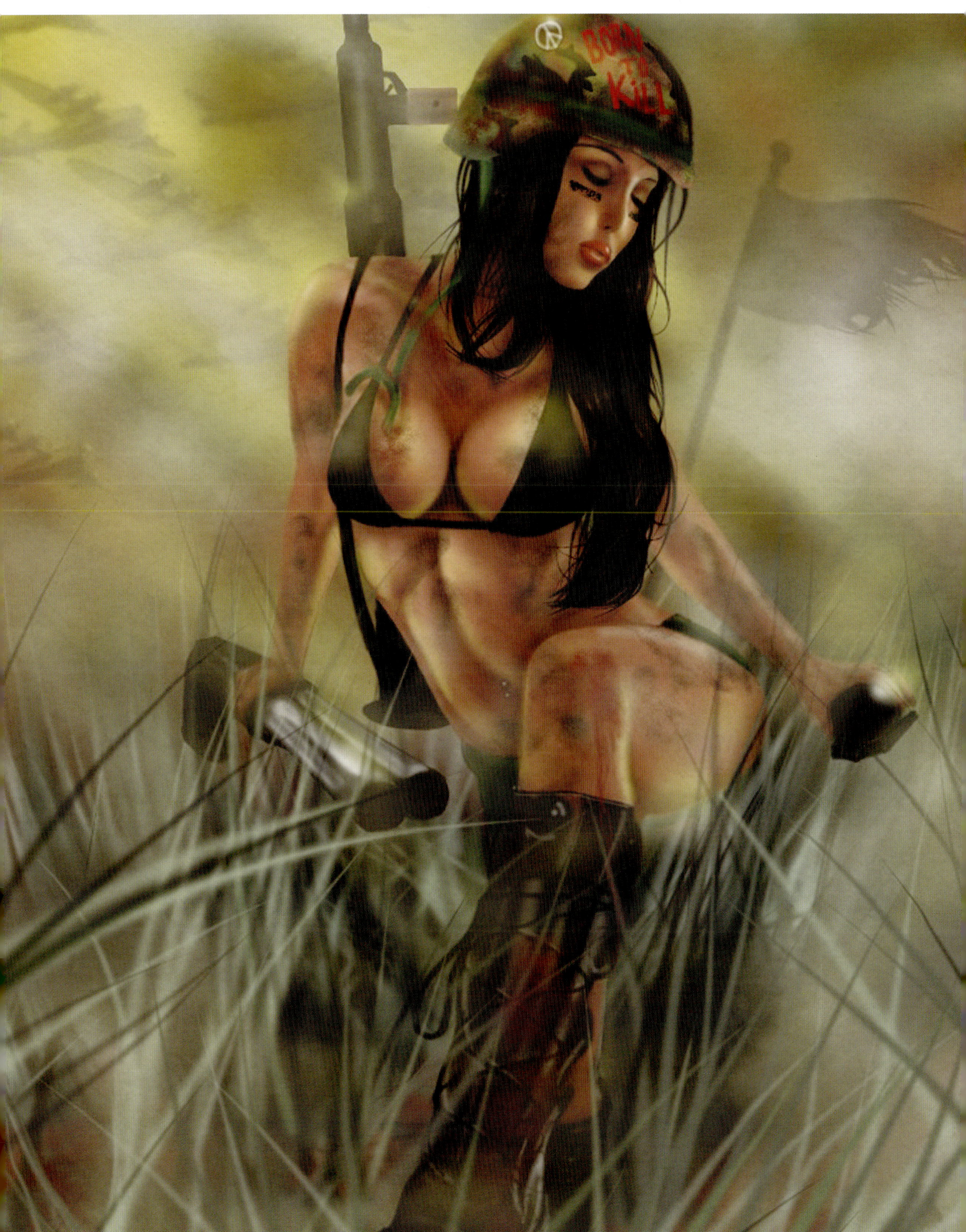


*Gimme Shelter*

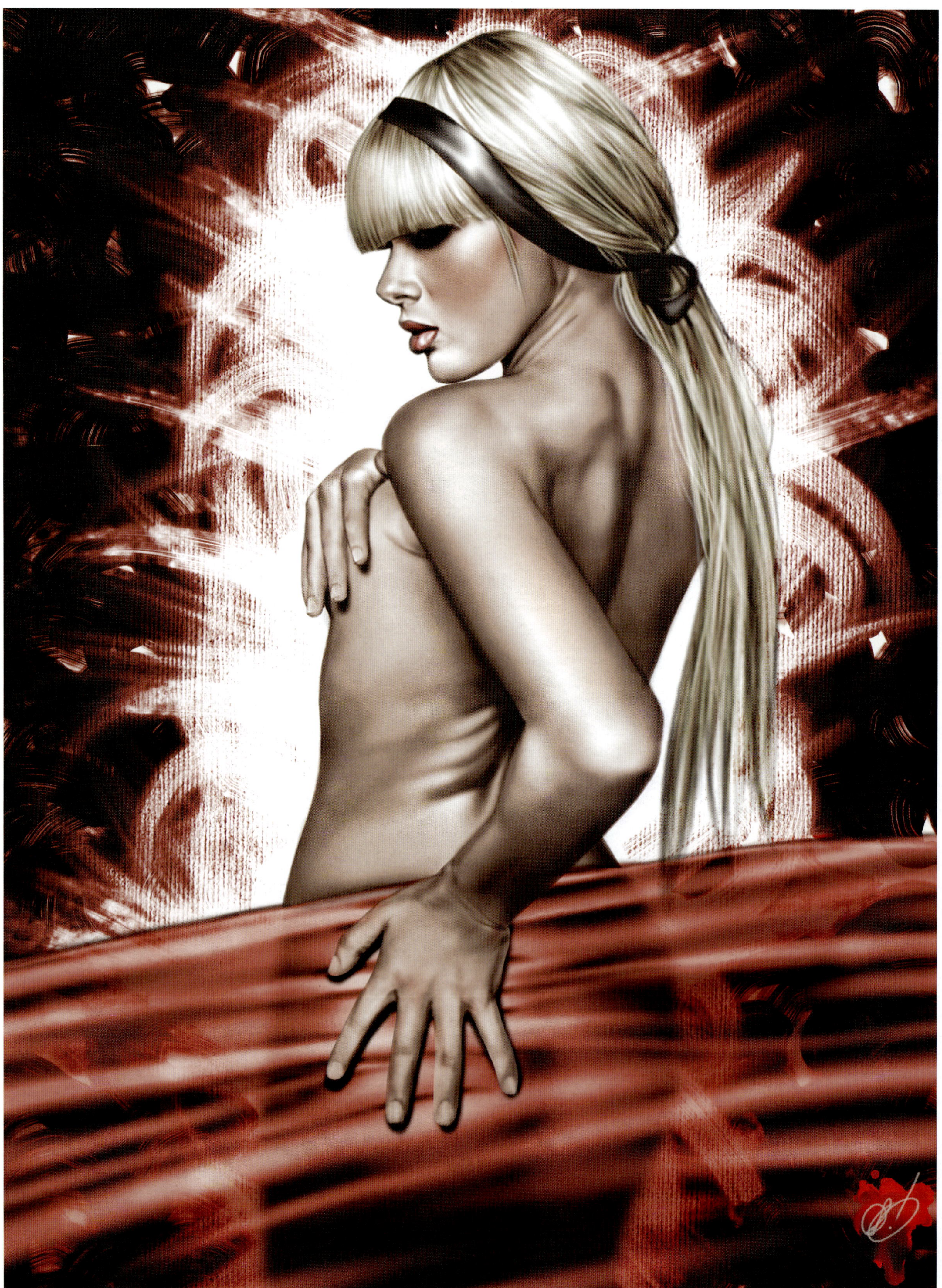

*Black and Red*

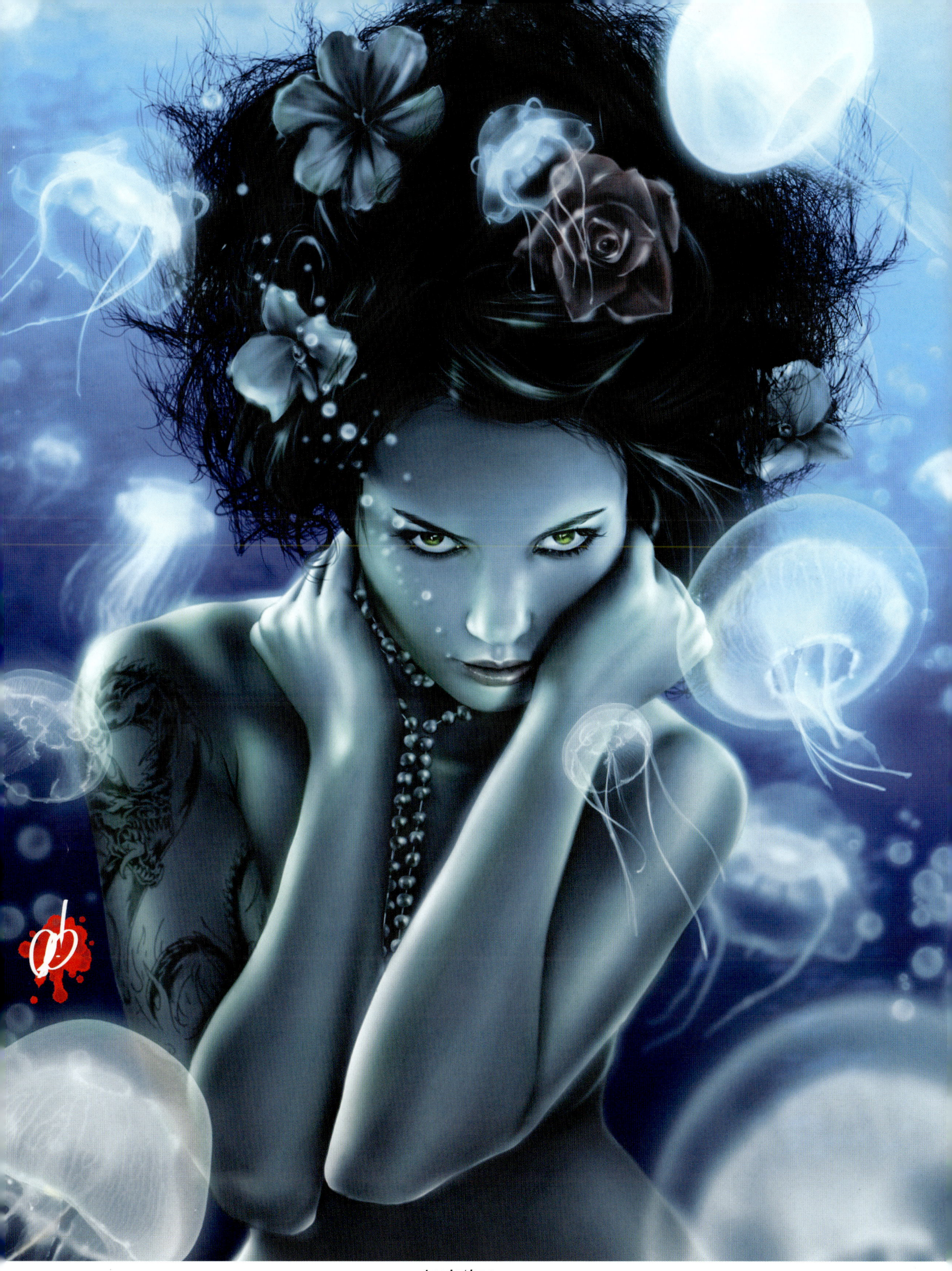

*Leviathan*

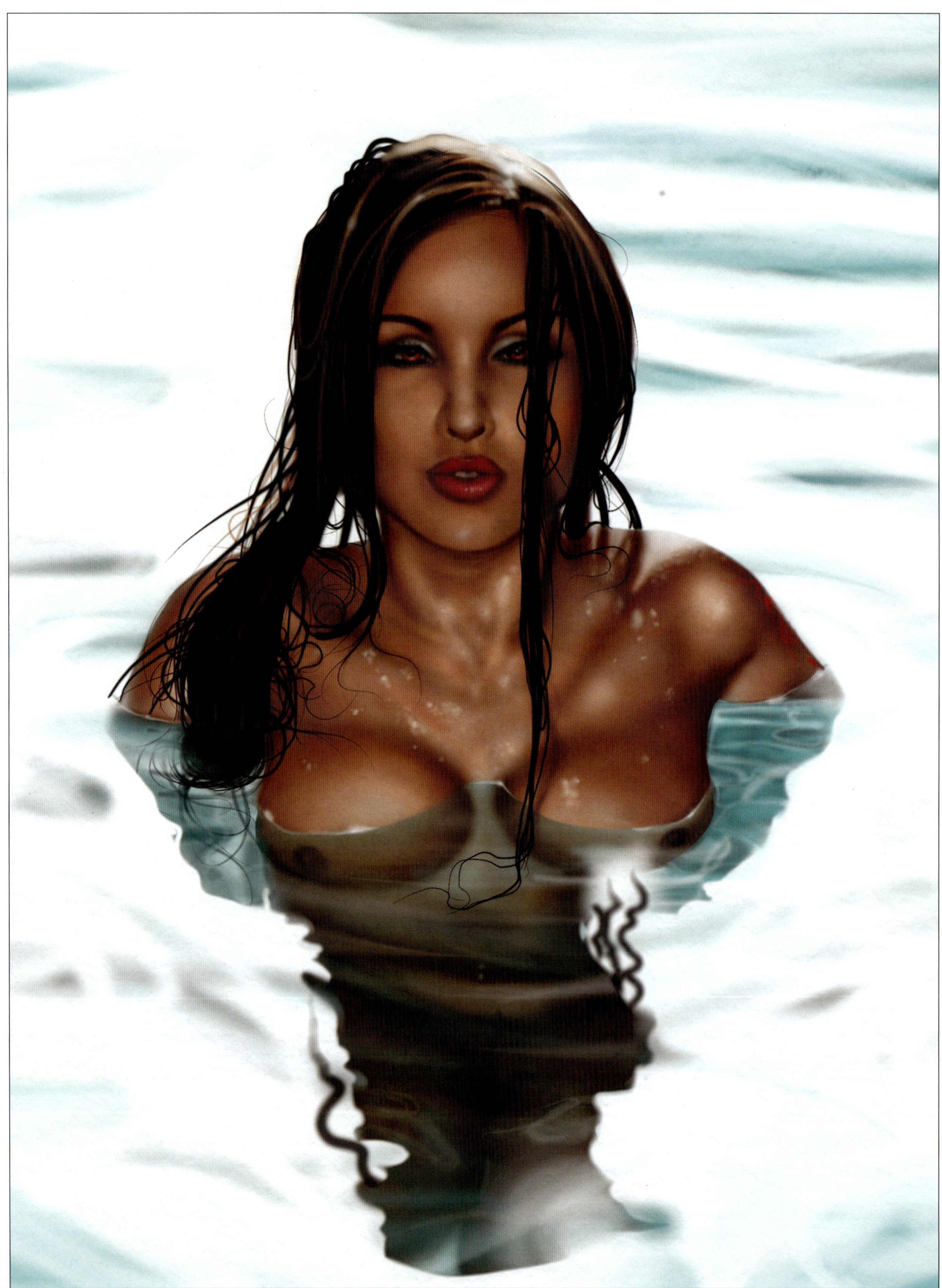

*La Llorona*

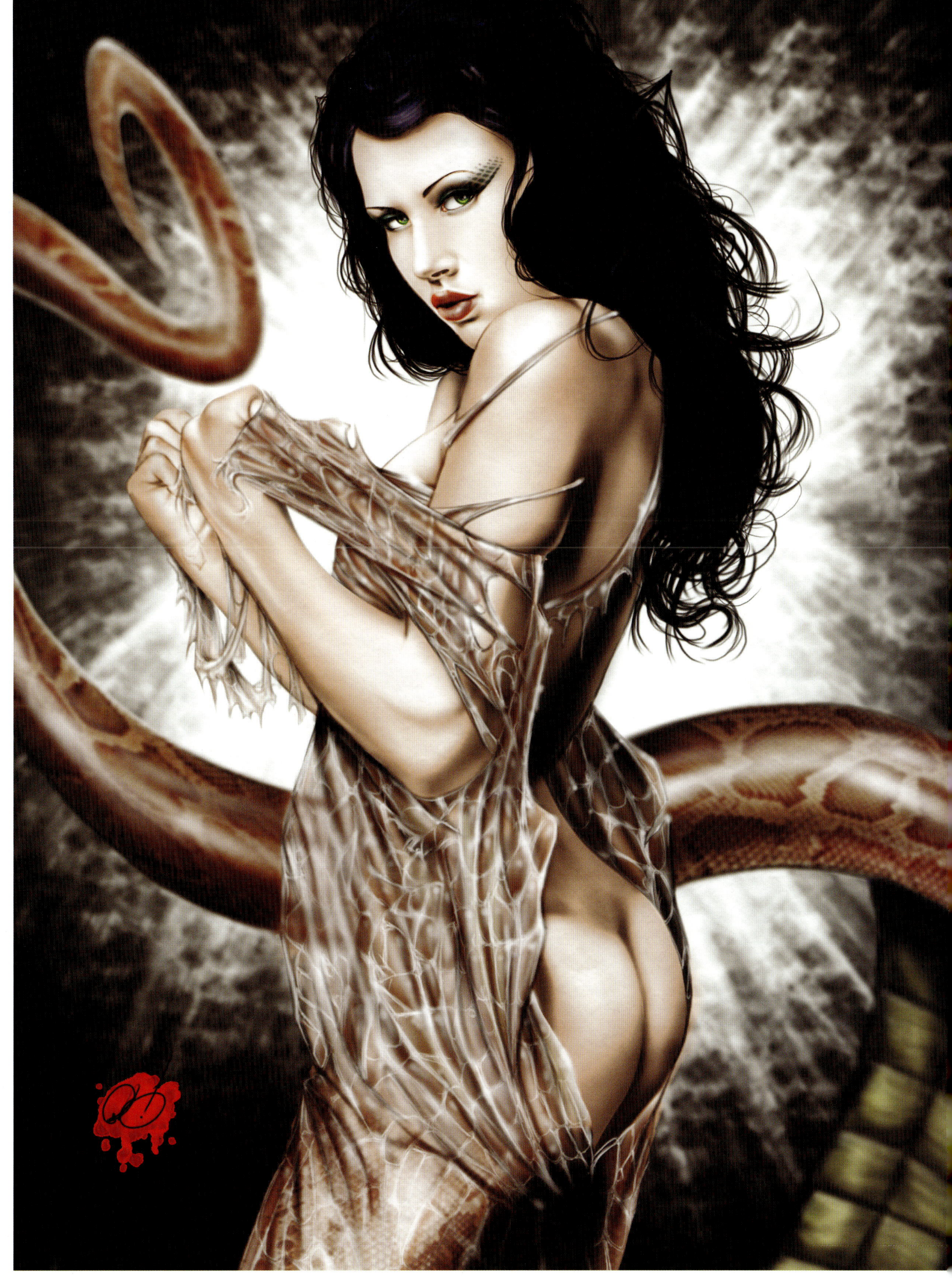

*Genesis 3:17*

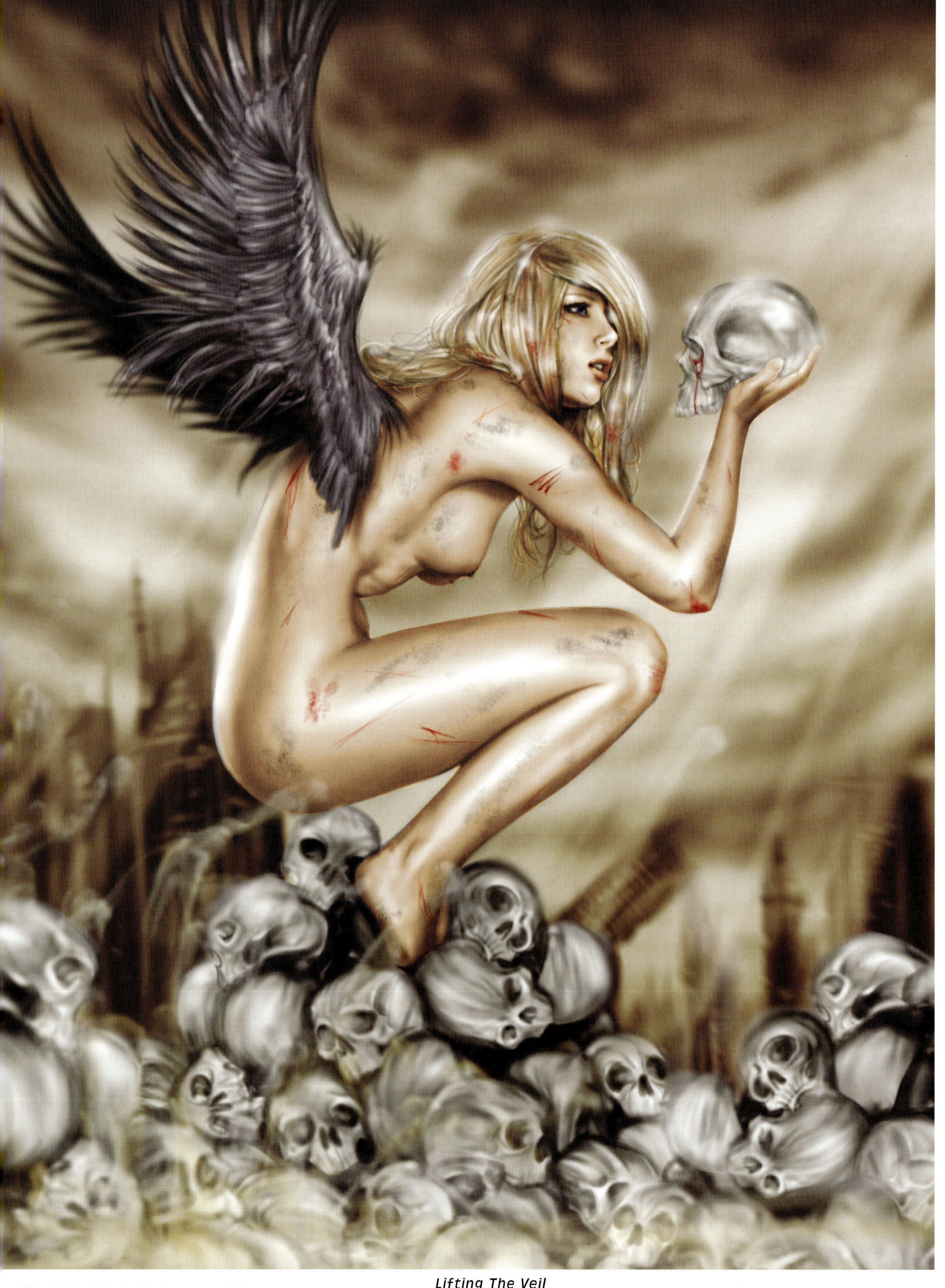

*Lifting The Veil*

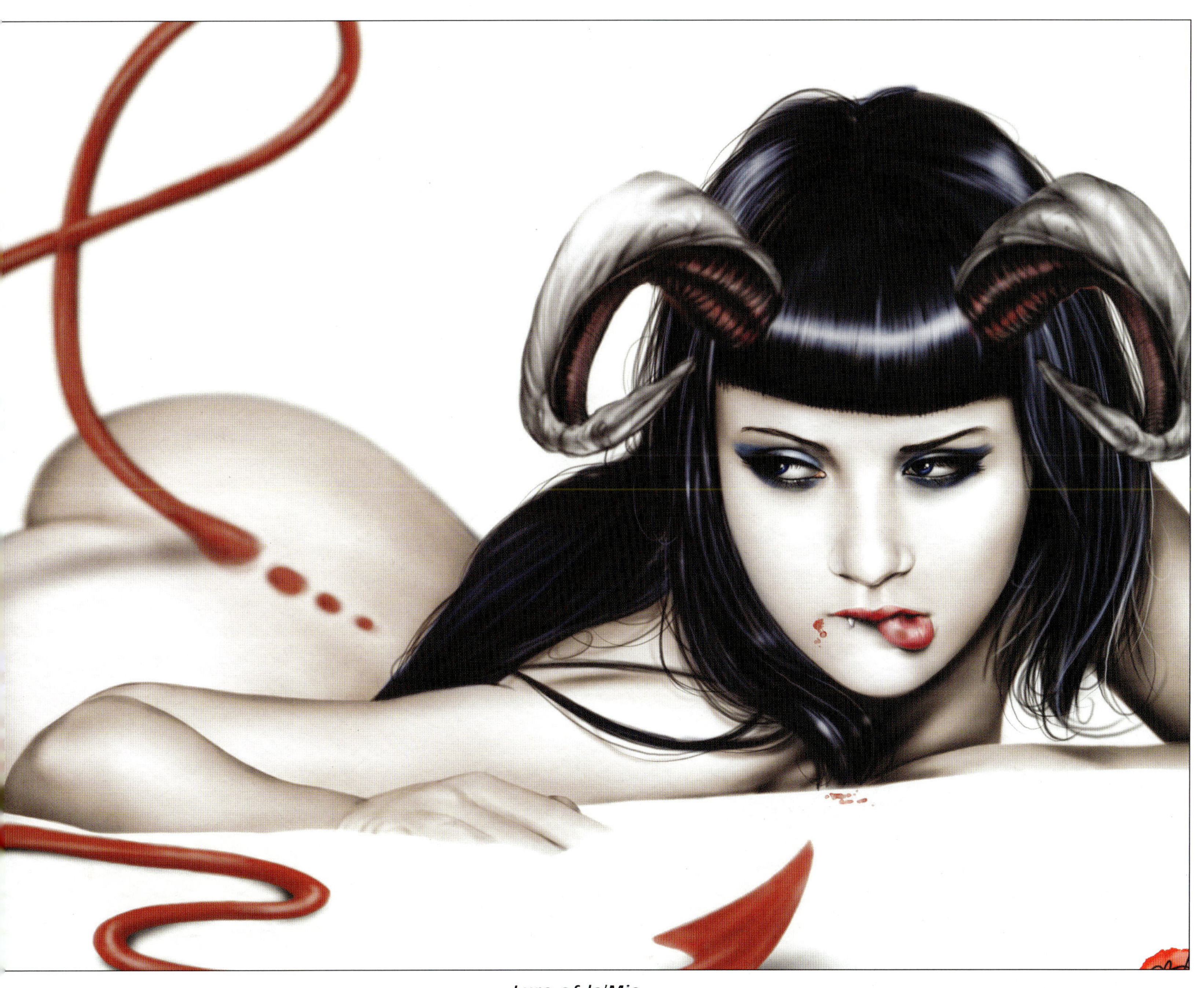

*Lure of la'Mia*

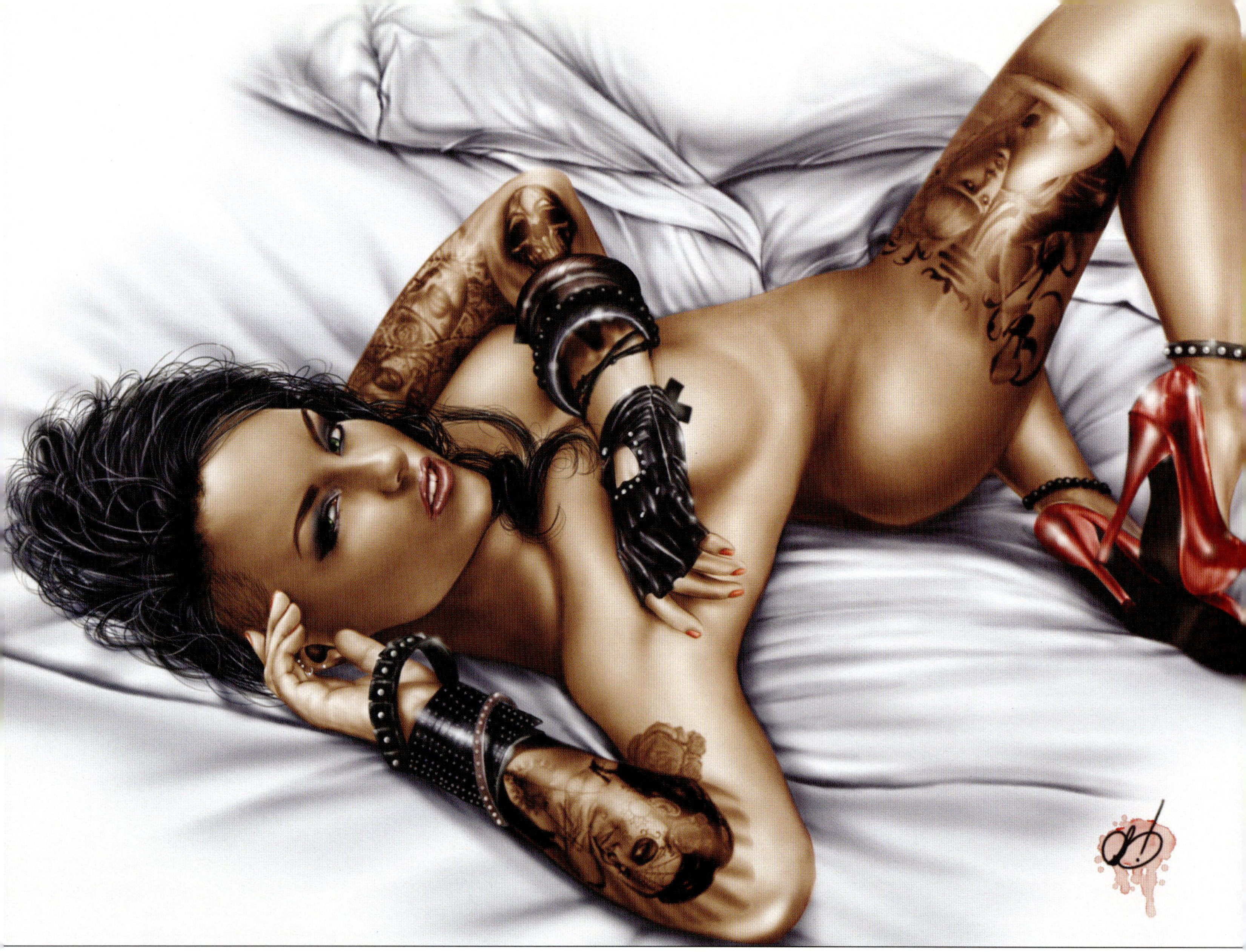

*Rock n Rolla*

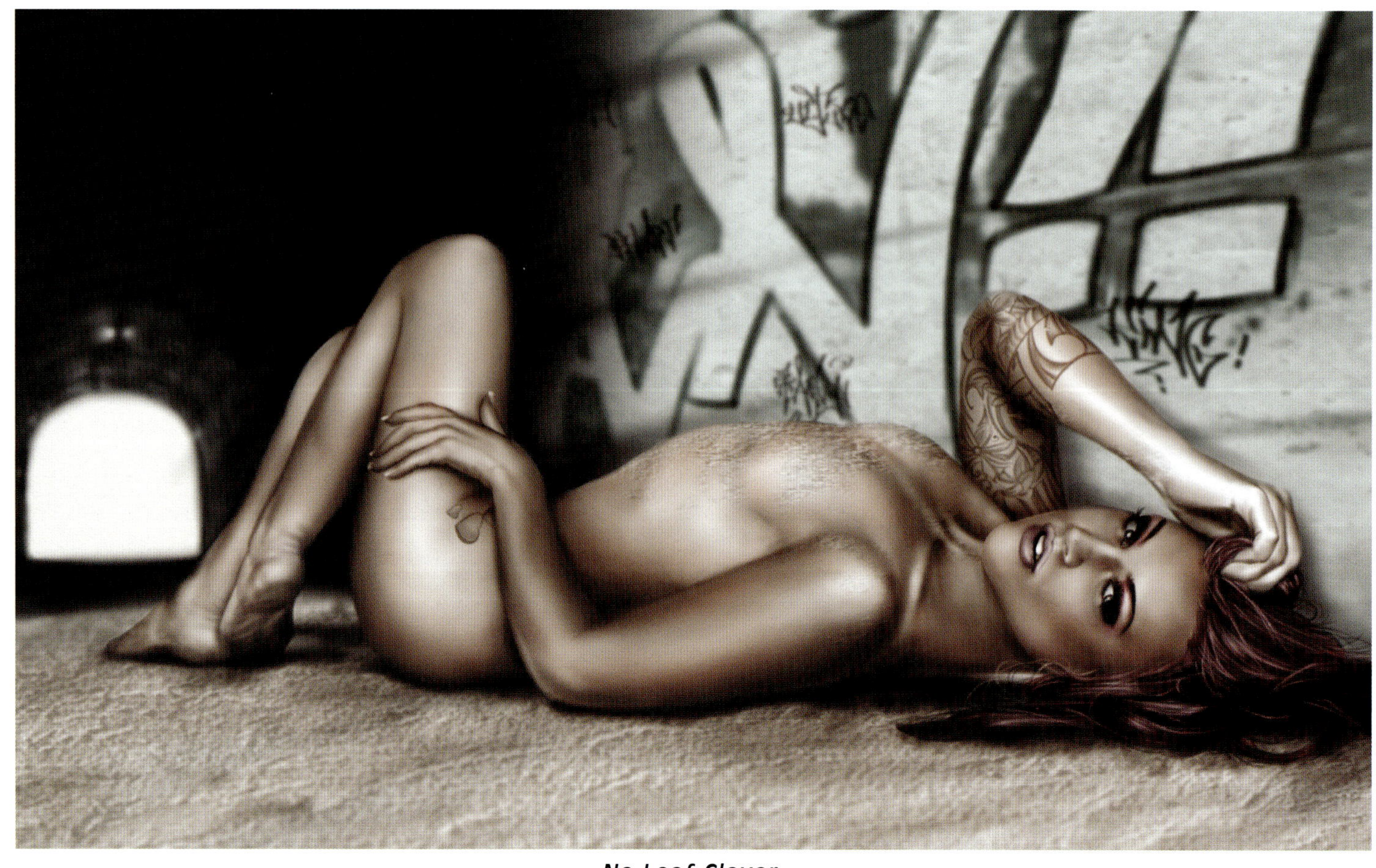

*No Leaf Clover*

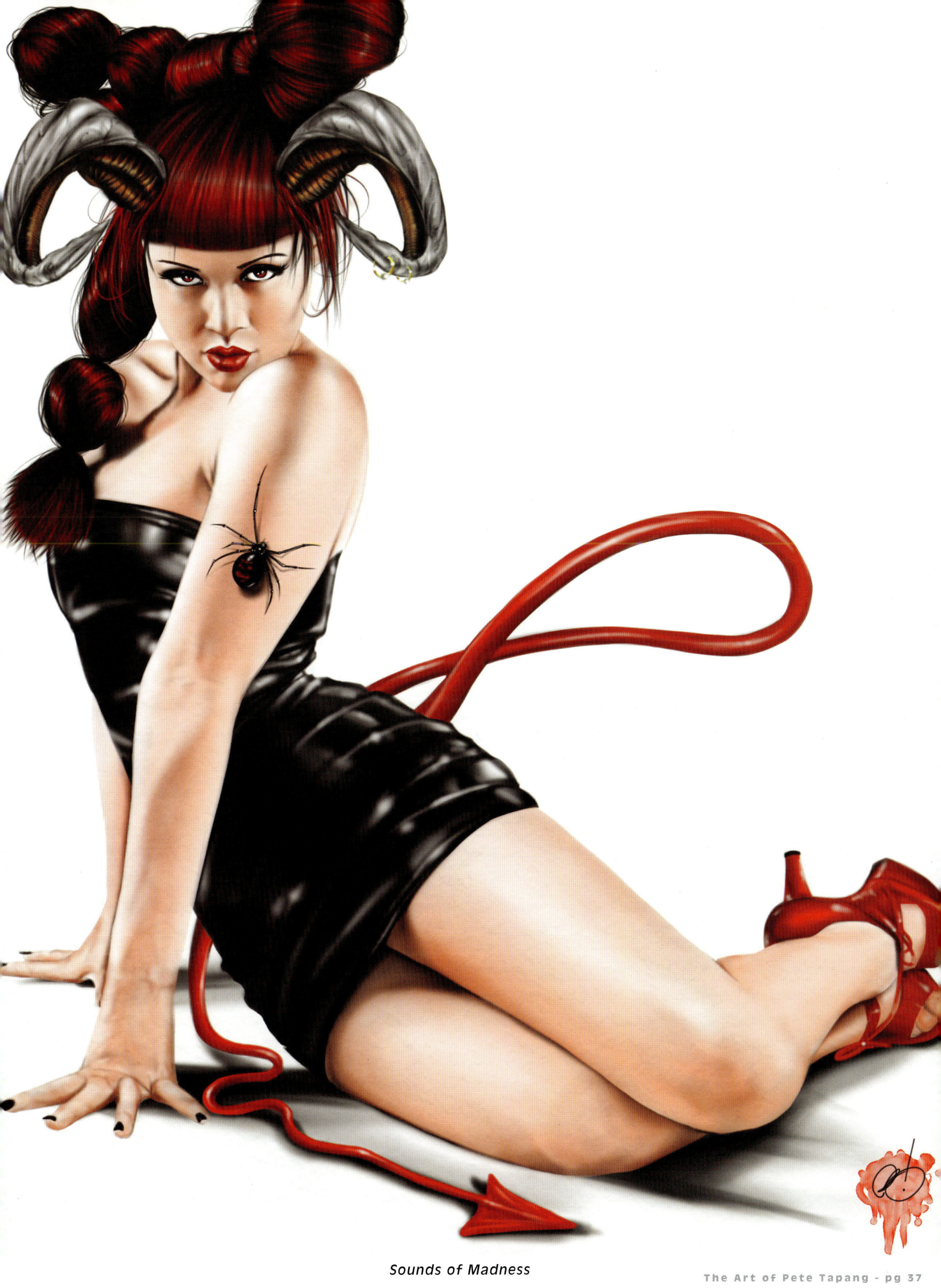

*Sounds of Madness*

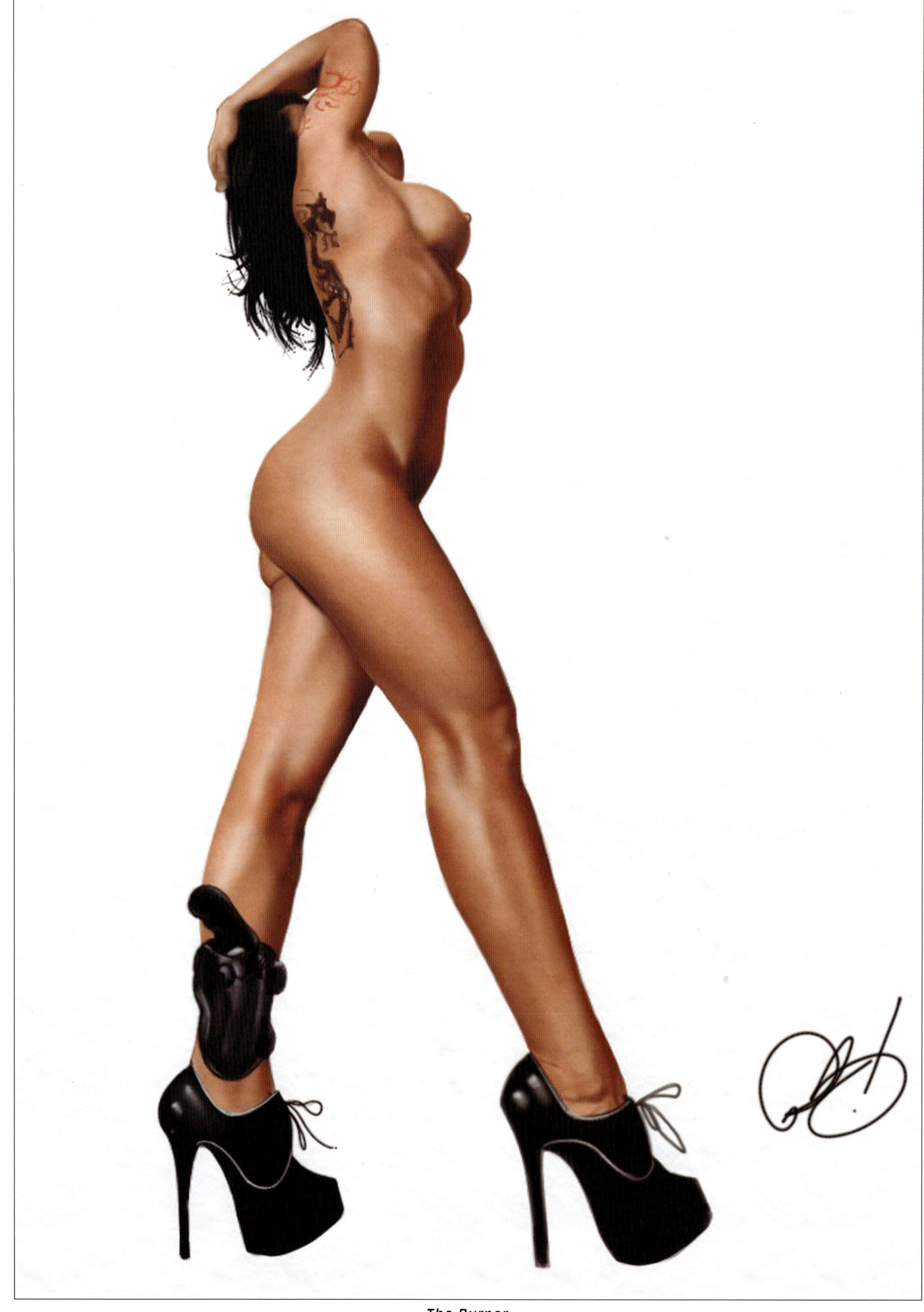

*The Burner*

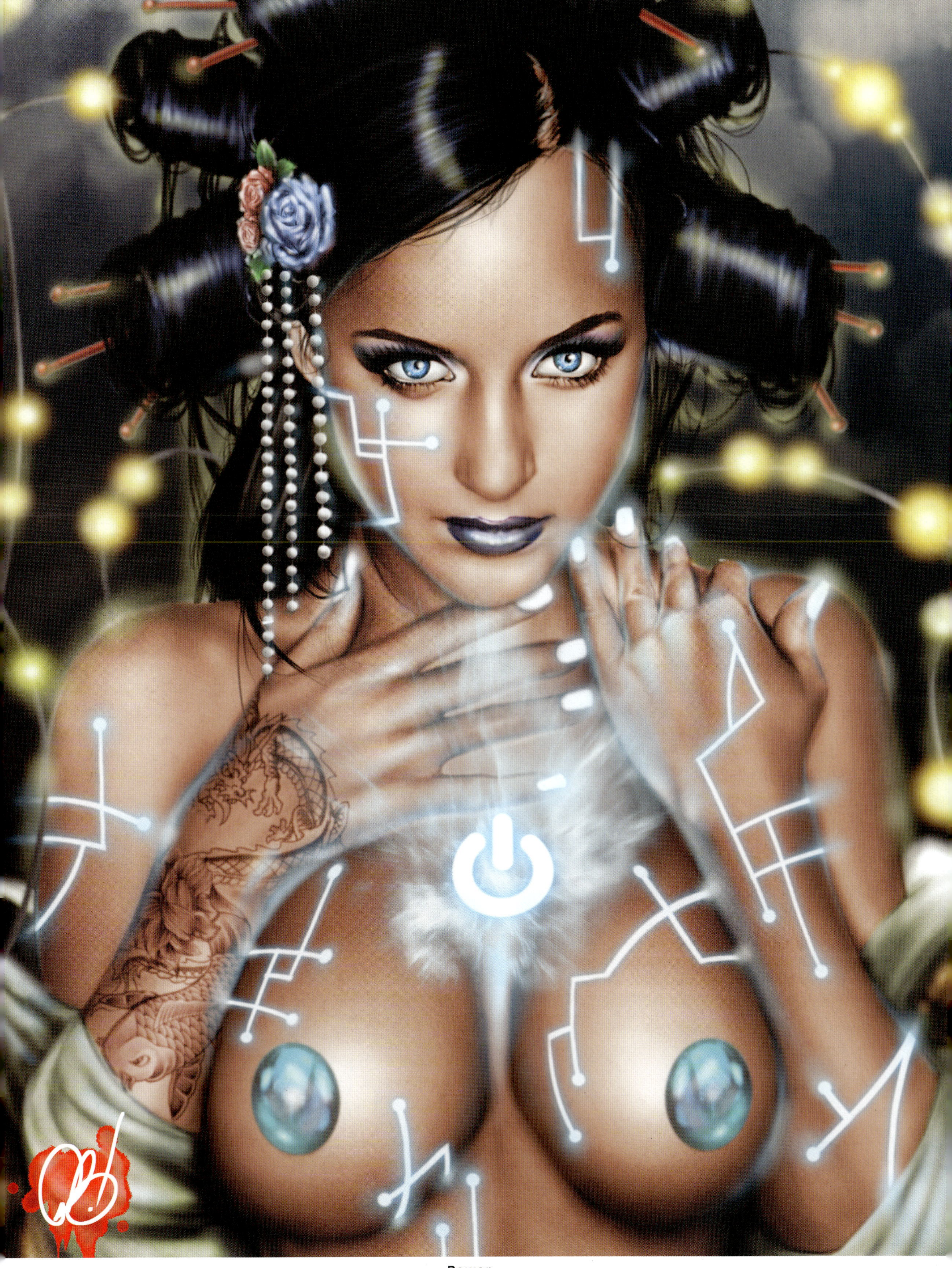

Power

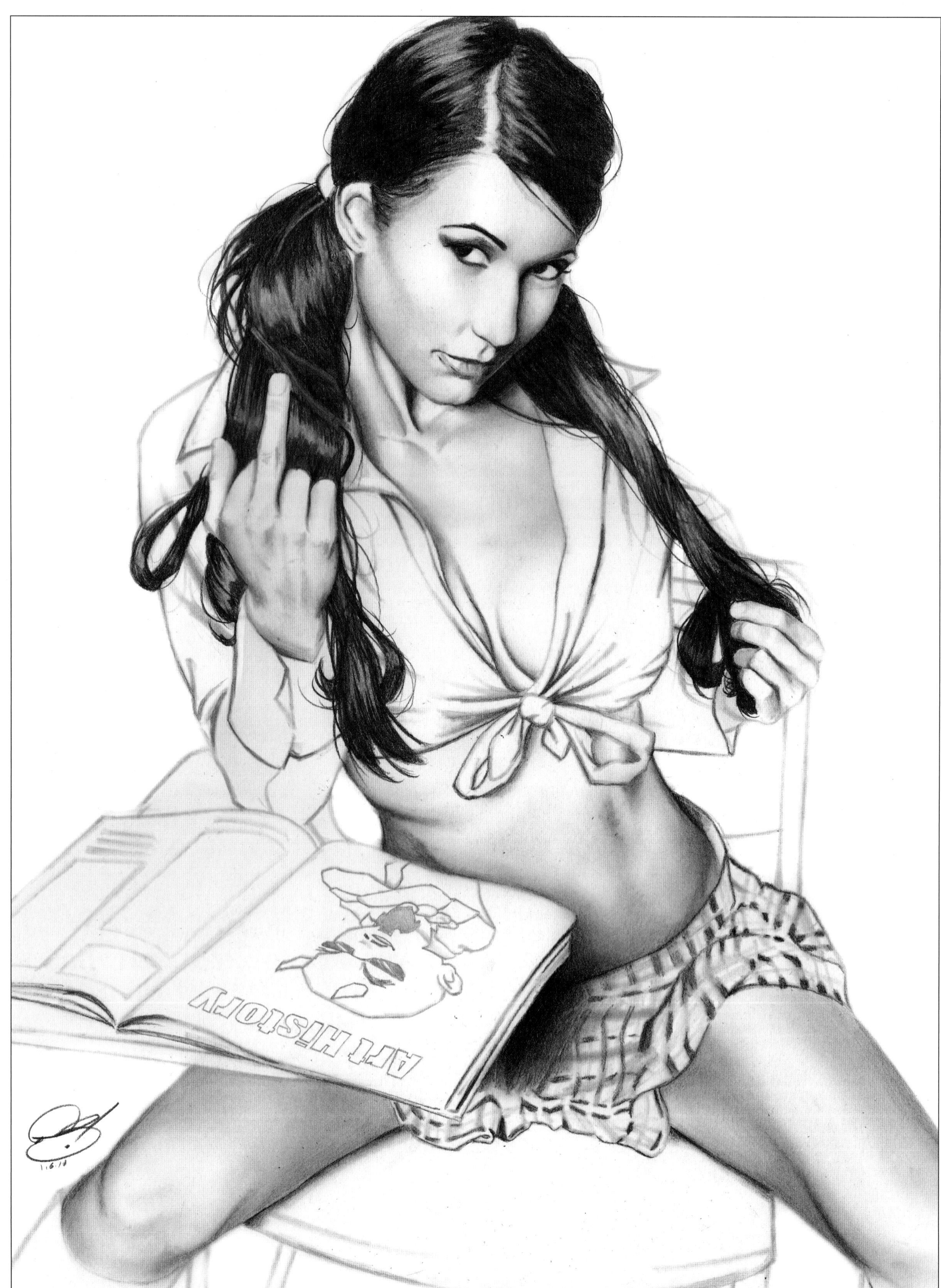


*Art History*

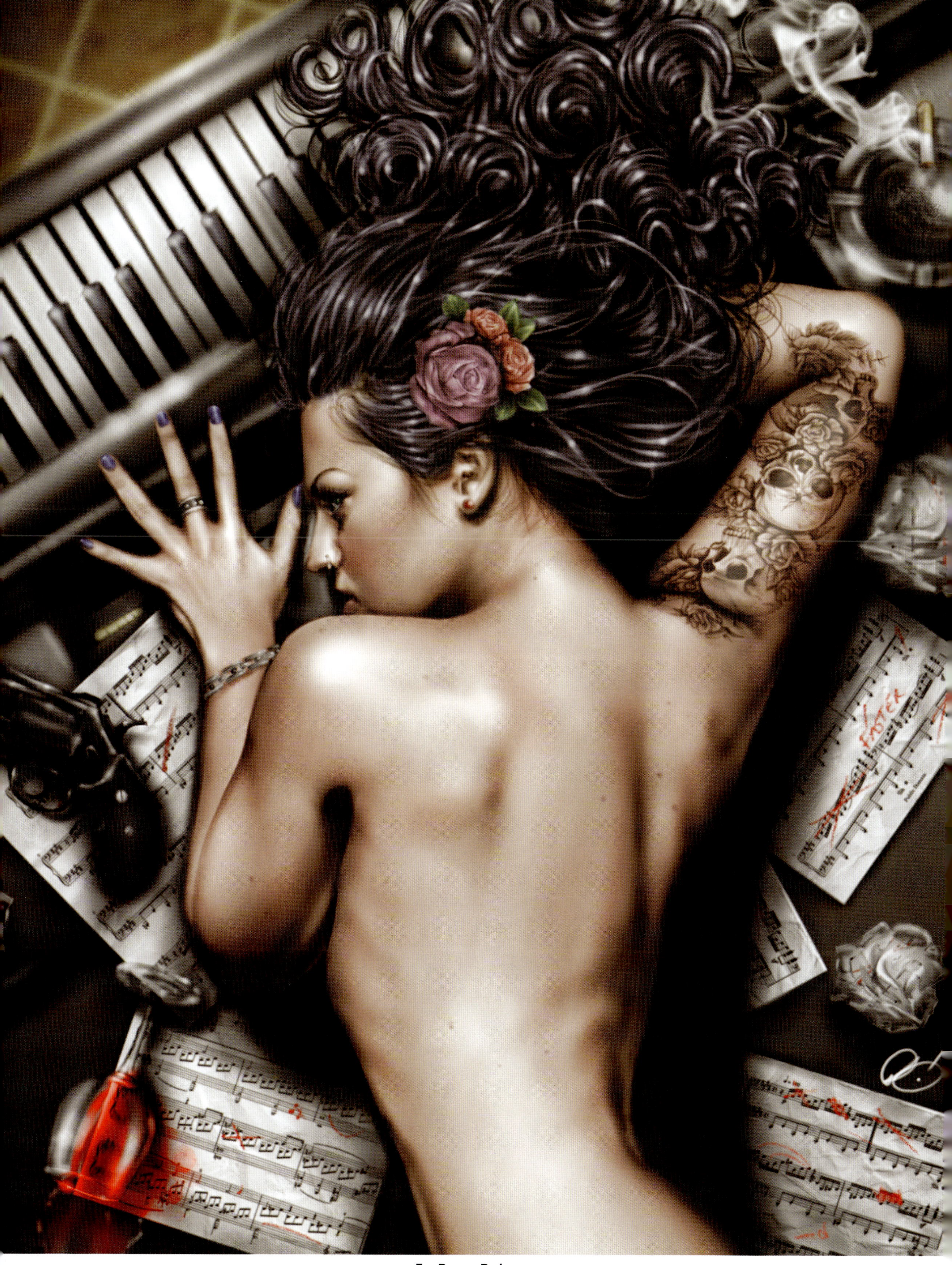

*Ex Dono Dei*

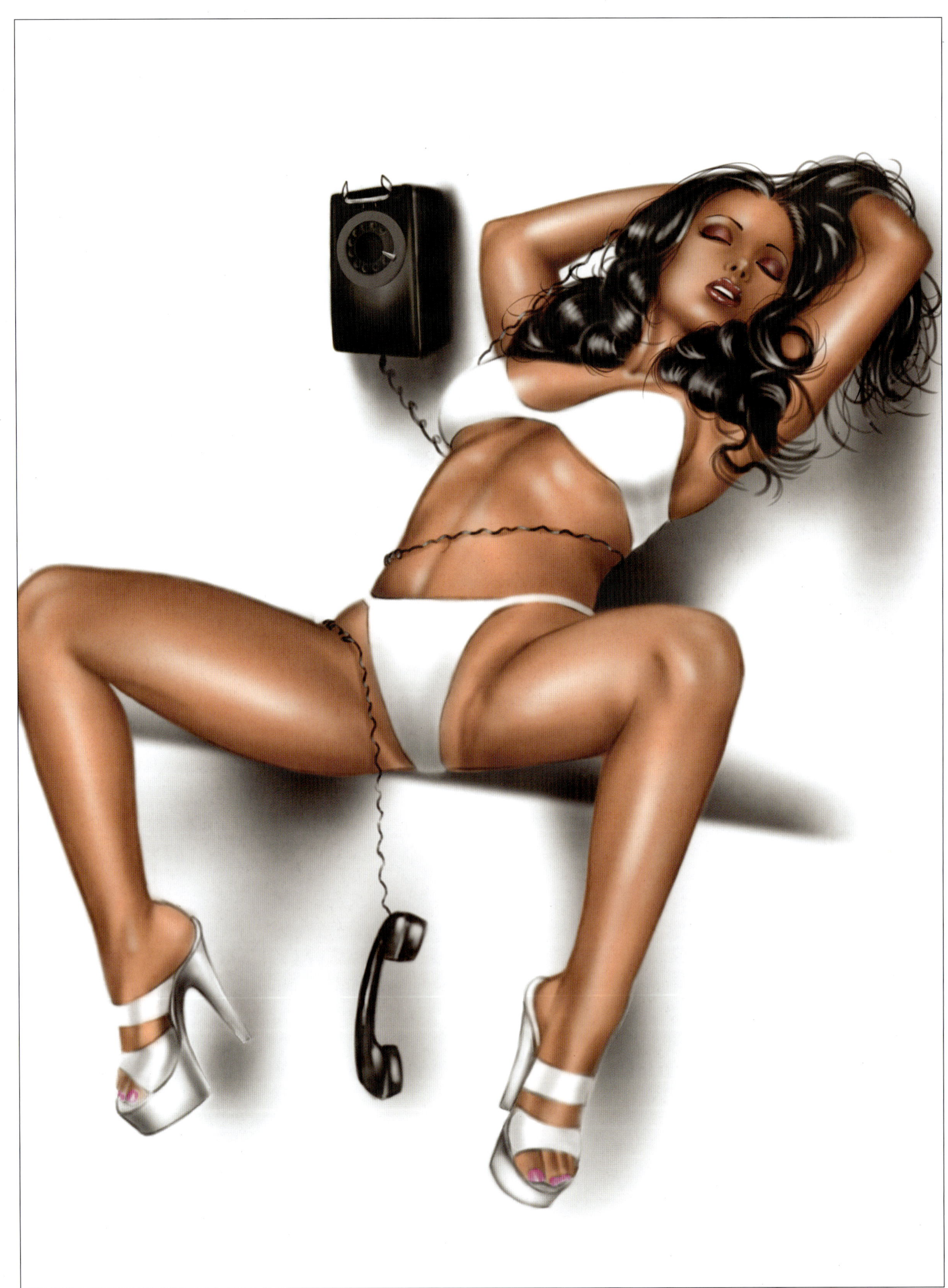

*Phone Sex Remix*

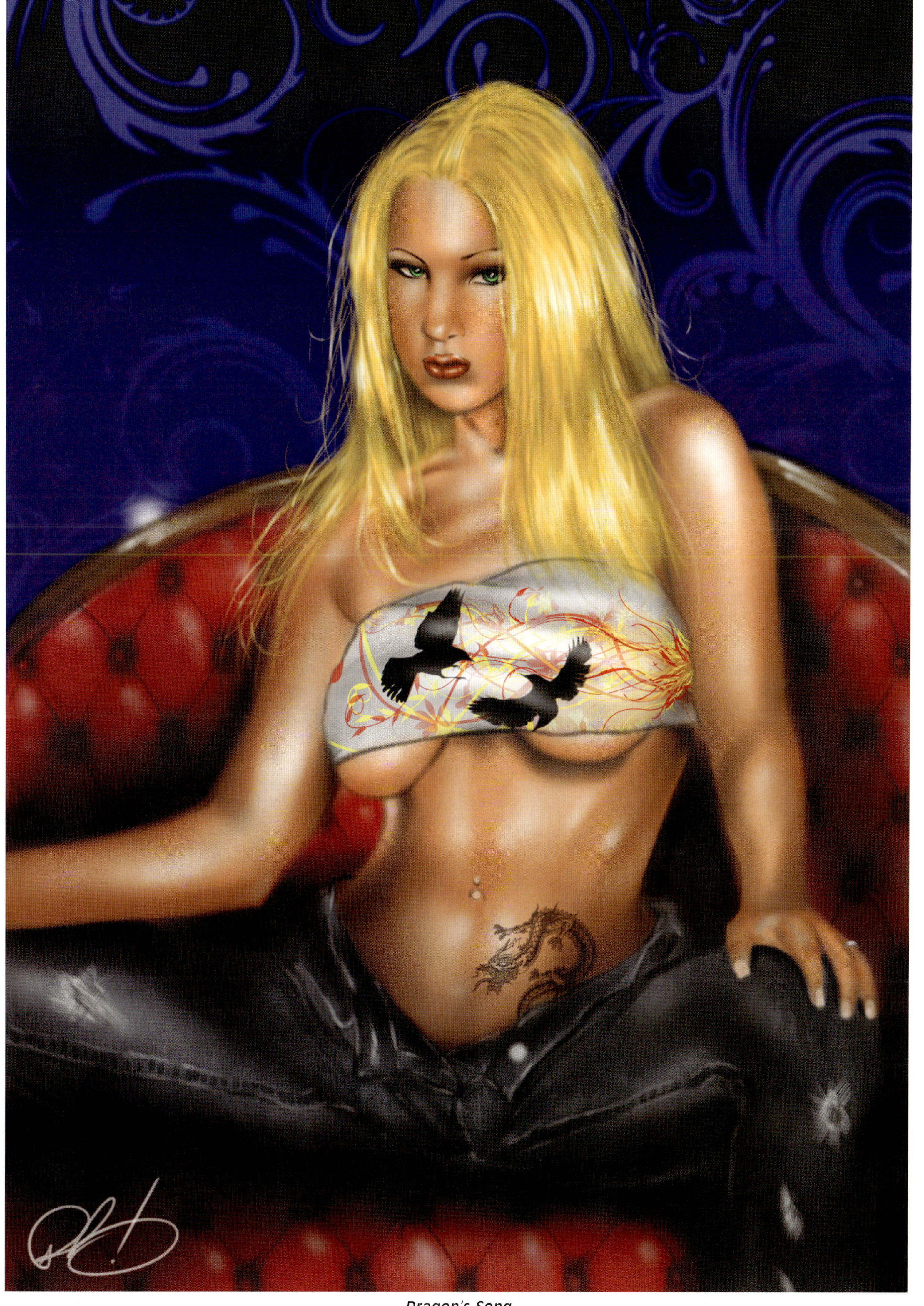

*Dragon's Song*

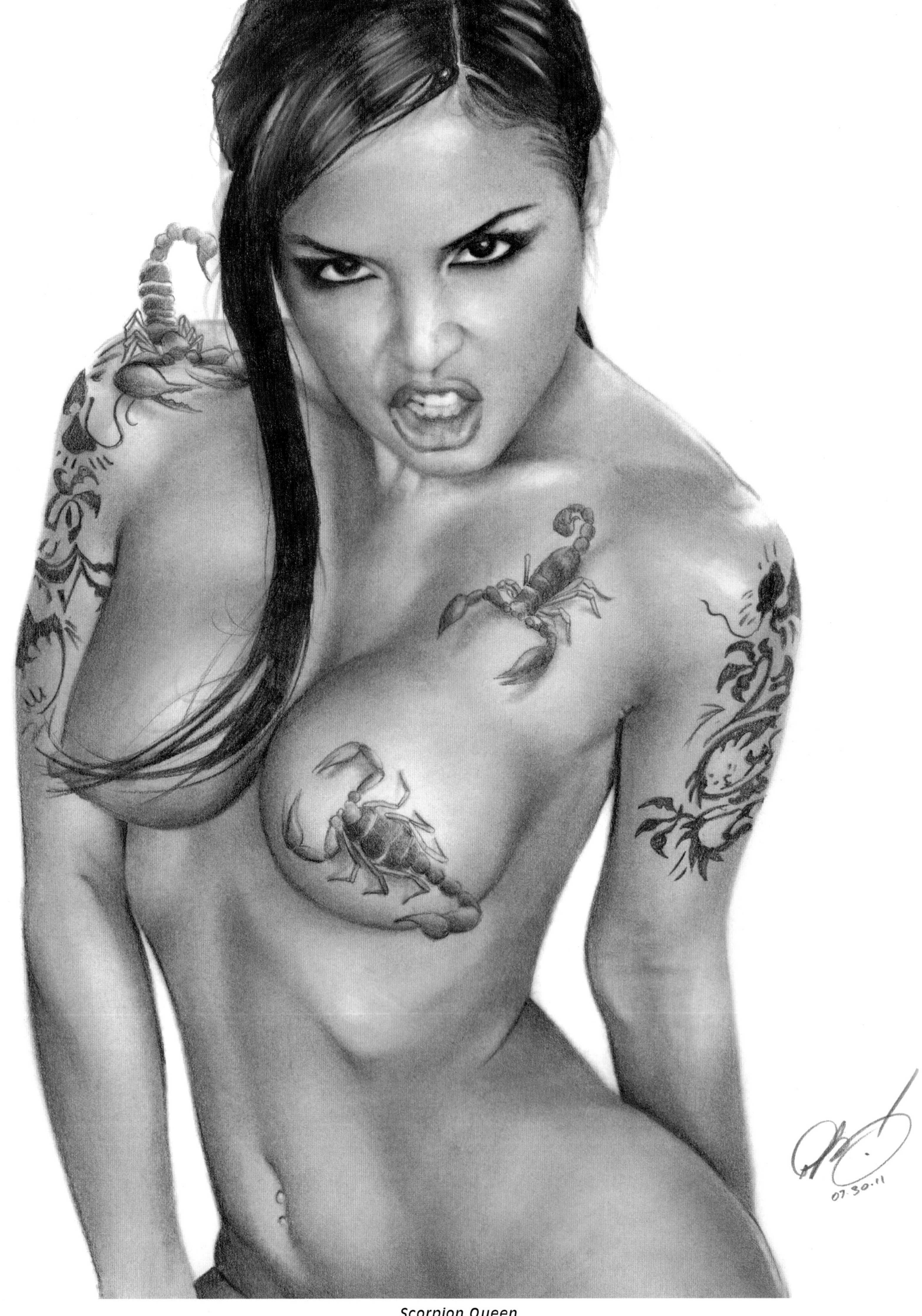


*Scorpion Queen*

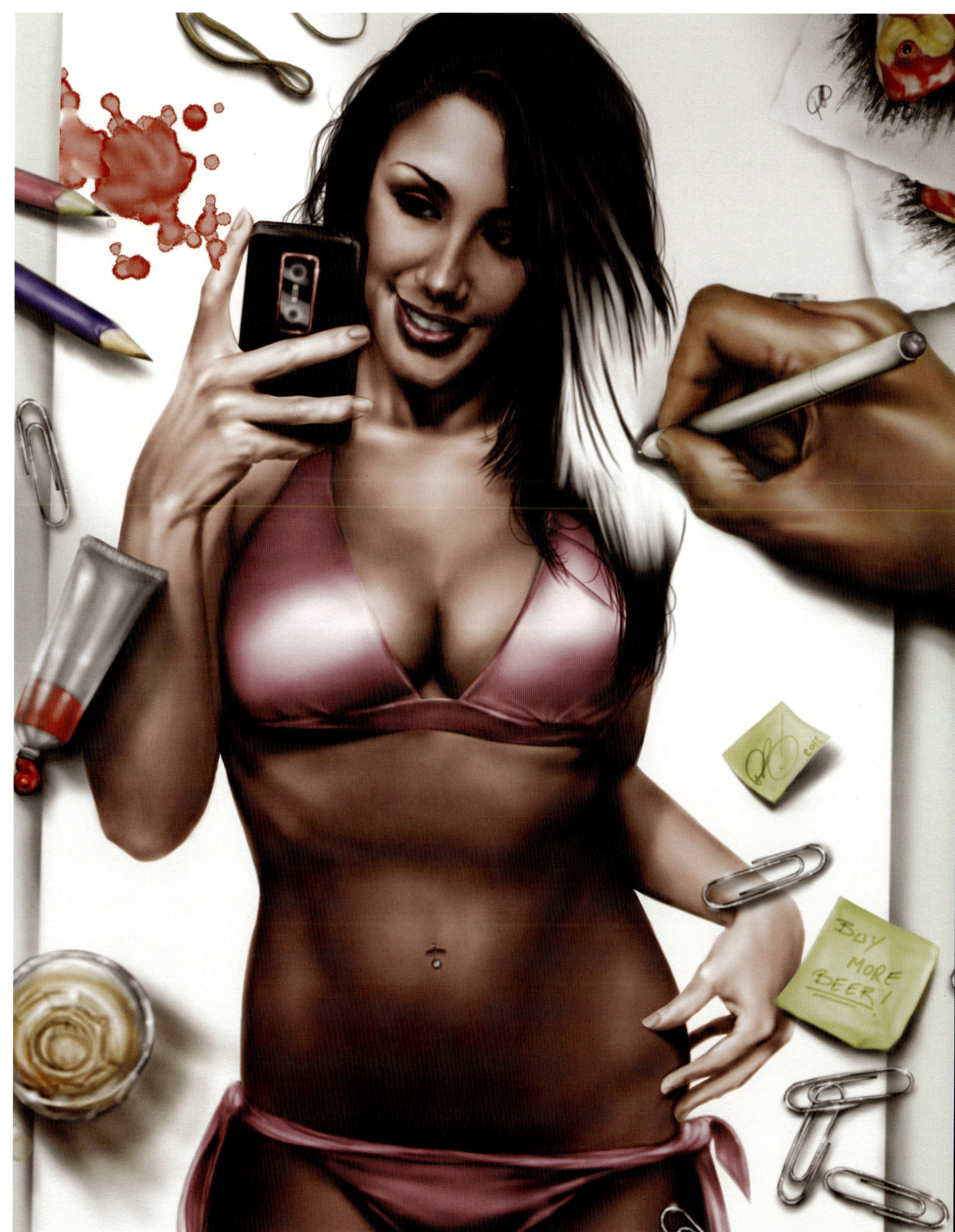


*A Day In The Life*

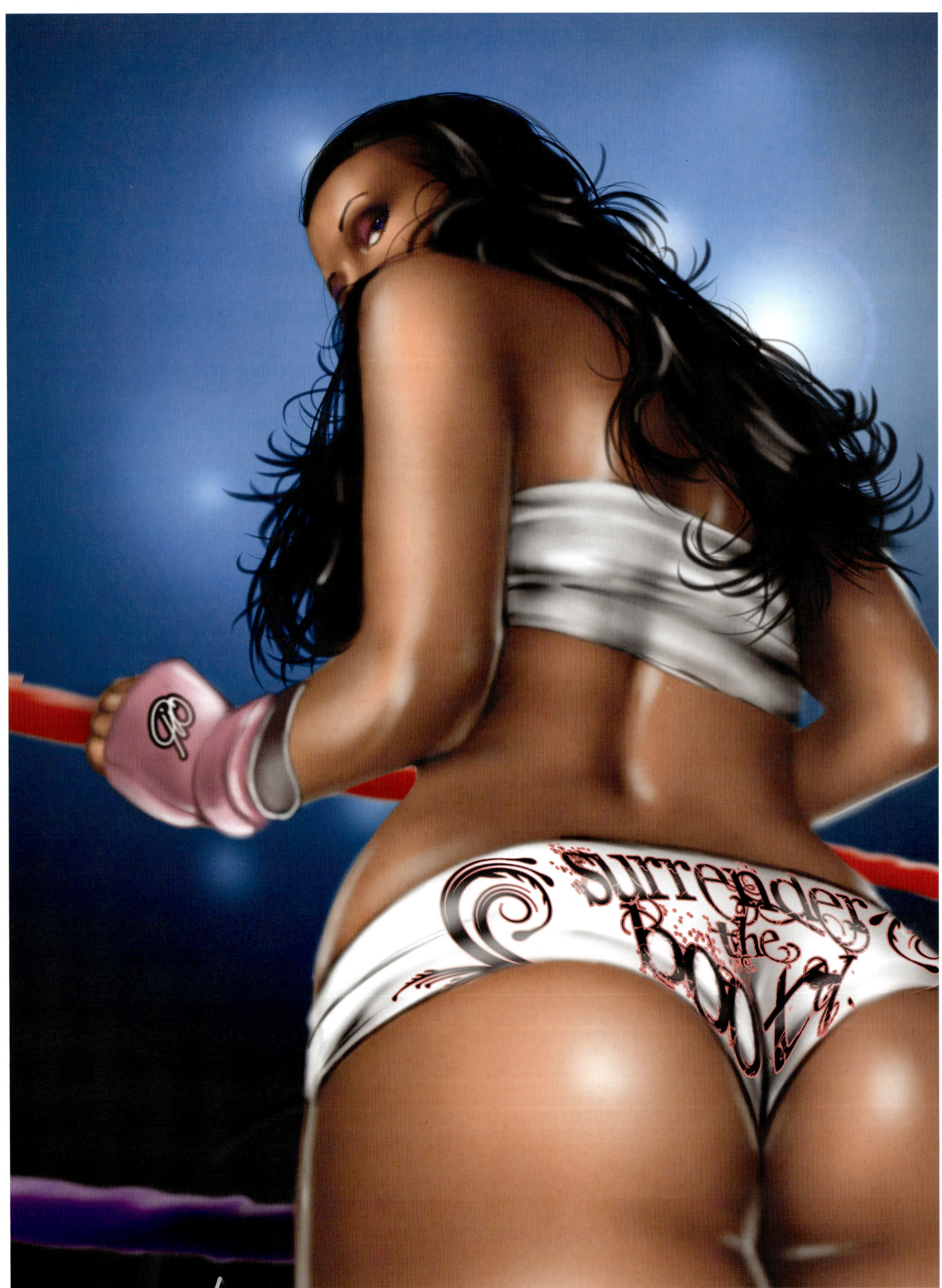


Surrender The Booty

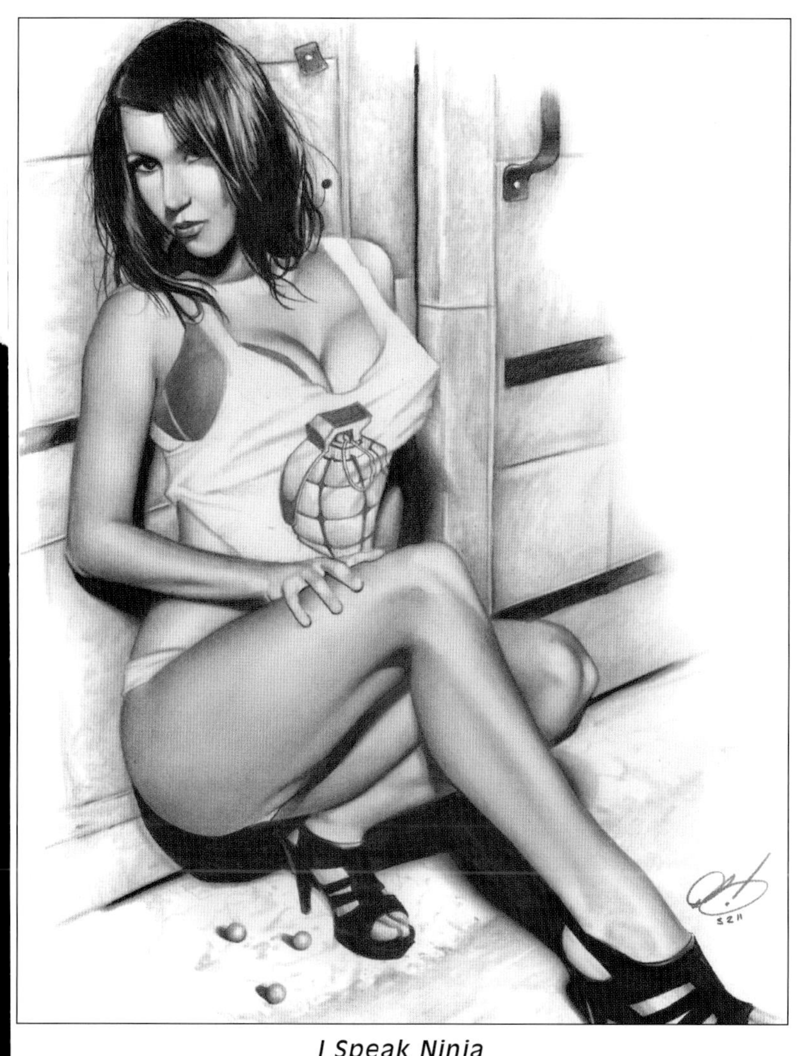

*I Speak Ninja*

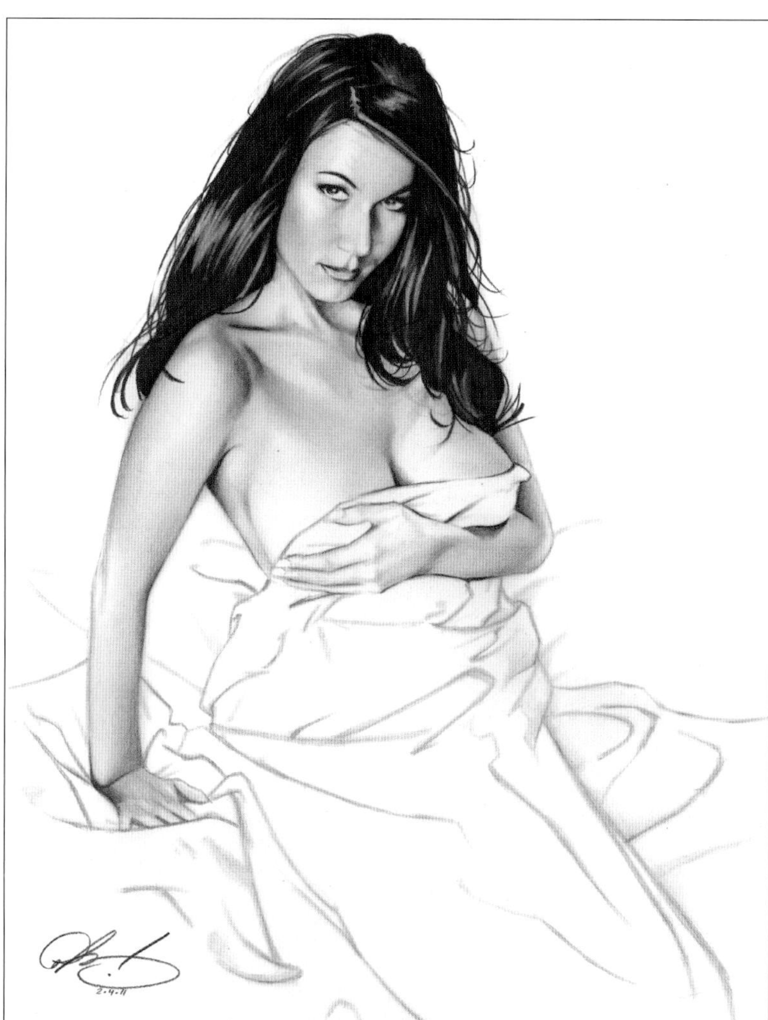

*Take On Me*

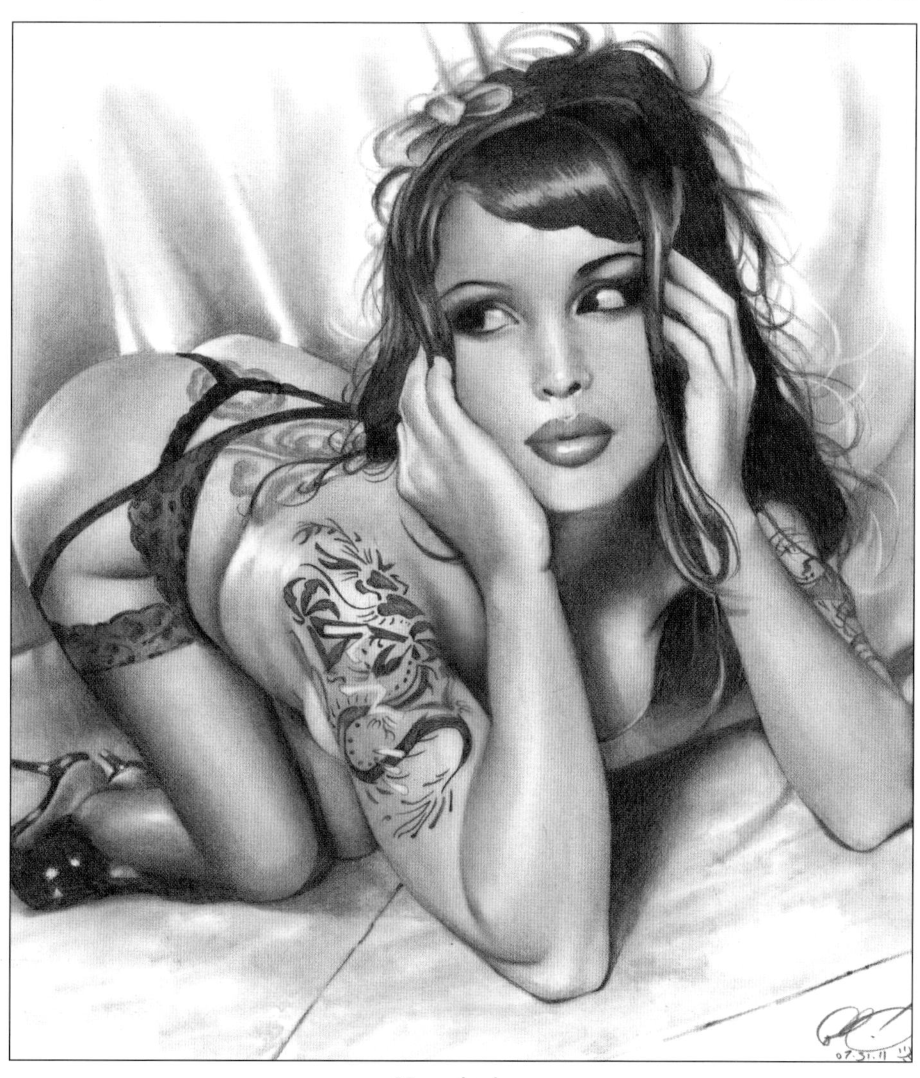

*Masuimi*

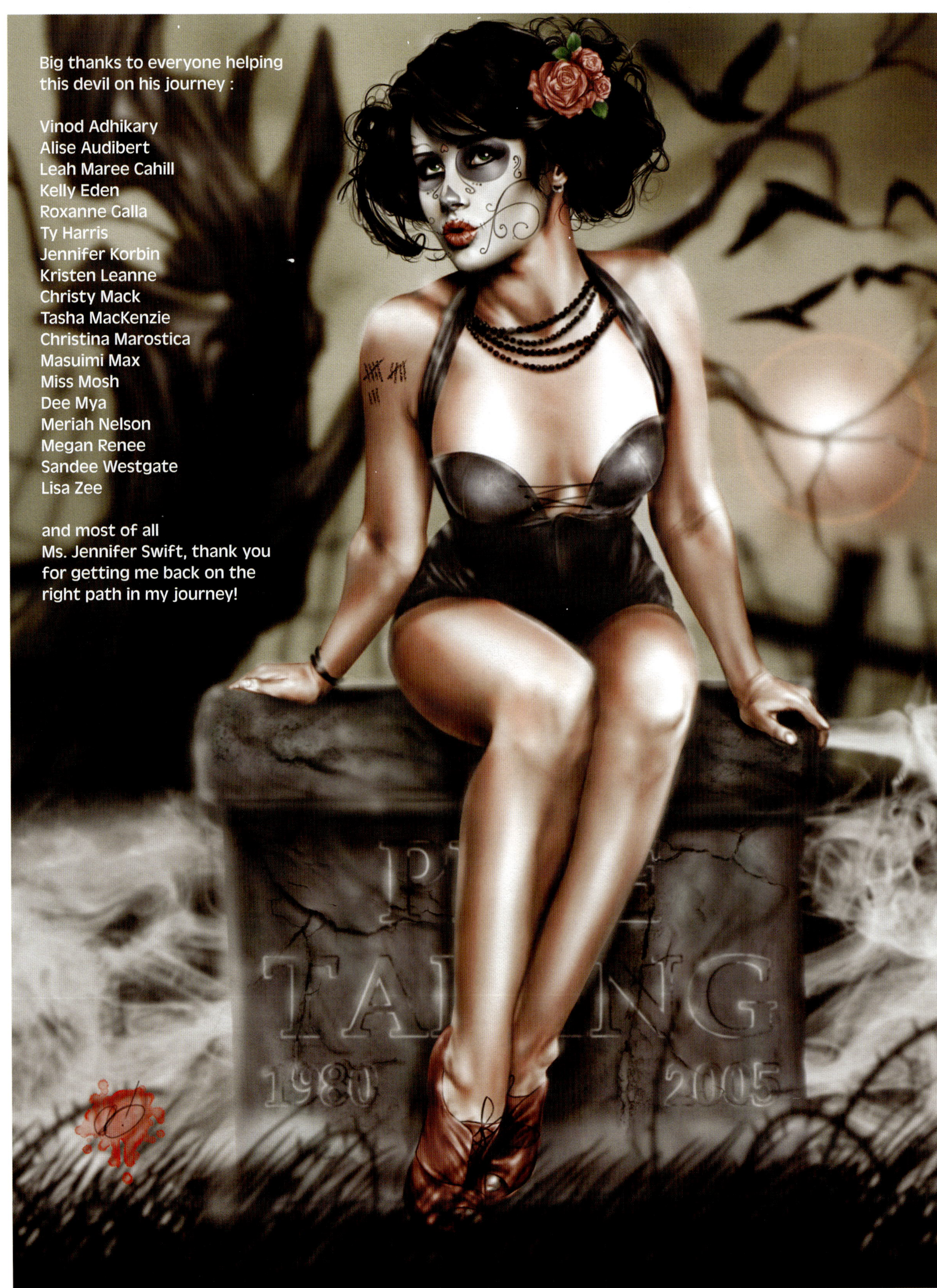


*The Deaths of Pete Tapang*